MW00584556

Heaven

Heaven

An Inkling of What's to Come

Myk Habets

CASCADE *Books* · Eugene, Oregon

HEAVEN
An Inkling of What's to Come

Cascade Books
An Imprint of Wipf and Stock Publishers
199 W. 8th Ave., Suite 3
Eugene, OR 97401

www.wipfandstock.com

PAPERBACK ISBN: 978-1-5326-3374-4
HARDCOVER ISBN: 978-1-5326-3376-8
EBOOK ISBN: 978-1-5326-3375-1

Cataloguing-in-Publication data:

Names: Habets, Myk.
Title: Heaven : an inkling of what's to come / Myk Habets.
Description: Eugene, OR : Cascade Books, 2018 | Includes bibliographical references and index.
Identifiers: ISBN 978-1-5326-3374-4 (paperback) | ISBN 978-1-5326-3376-8 (hardcover) | ISBN 978-1-5326-3375-1 (ebook)
Subjects: LCSH: Heaven—Christianity. | Future life—Christianity.
Classification: BT846.3 H11 2018 (print) | BT846.3 (ebook)

Manufactured in the U.S.A.

To my son Liam, now also my brother in Christ.
Mischievous, athletic, bold, funny, caring, and fun. I am proud of you and I love you.

To my daughter Sydney, now also my sister in Christ.
Caring, compassionate, gentle, artistic, fun-loving, and courageous. I love you and I am proud of you.

And to my nieces and nephews.

Those in the faith:
Amy, Joshua, Taylor, Yanka, Chantelle, Fraser, Jade, Matt, and Breanne.

And those on the way to faith:
Caleb, Riley, Isabella, and Mayah.

May all the joys of eternal life be yours.

Contents

Acknowledgments ix

1. Introduction: An Inkling of What's to Come 1
2. The Best of All Possible Worlds (What Is Heaven Like?) 12
3. Raised Immortal (What Will We Be Like in the Resurrection?) 36
4. An Endless Adventure (What Will We Do in the New Jerusalem?) 58
5. A Great Cloud of Witnesses (Who Will Be in Zion?) 81
6. Conclusion: On Eating Pie in the Sky 98

Study Guides 113
Select Bibliography 125
Topical Index 129

Acknowledgments

This book, perhaps more than any other I have written, is the product of a family—a family of faith. God obviously designed family to be a laboratory of learning, both for children and parents. I have learnt more from my wife and children than I could ever garner from books and libraries. I often say that my two children are my most astute and theologically capable students. This book is especially dedicated to them. And, of course, what I learnt from my own mum, dad, and sister is immeasurable. Initially dragged along to children's church as a young boy, encouraged into youth group as a teenager, and willingly participating in church as an adult, my parents have been a constant encouragement in my Christian walk.

Thank you to the many children and their parents who spoke with me about this project. I am especially grateful for the questions children were asking about heaven. Out of the mouths of babes . . . (Matt 21:16).

Without many years of lecturing to undergraduate and graduate classes at Carey Baptist College and Graduate School, my ability to navigate the heady waters of biblical eschatology would have been severely lacking. Teaching MB6/724, Humanity and Hope, to successive classes of students has been a privilege and a delight. Much of the material in this book has been unleashed on classes of unsuspecting students and there it found an astute audience and a home. While the questions posed in this book are from the lips of children, they are no less profound, and often no different, from the questions adult learners ask. That is why this book is for all of us.

I am deeply thankful for the many people who have read all or parts of this book in draft stages and made critical comments on it. Karen Warner (children's worker extraordinaire), our Family Life Group at Windsor Park Baptist Church, and other friends paid me the high honor of being candid and honest with me about the readability of what I was putting before them. If this book is a stinker, I blame them.

Once again, a special thank you goes to Sarah Snell for her eye for detail, enthusiasm for editing work, and her efficiency in getting the job done. You make publishing much easier for me, Sarah, and I thank you for that. I also hope that your own children might benefit from what I have written here as I have benefitted from their questions.

To the good people at Wipf and Stock/Cascade Books. You have befriended many authors and scholars, you put on a great reception each year at the AAR/SBL annual conference, and you make people feel like they matter. Chris Spinks, thank you for your unbridled enthusiasm for this work and for seeing it through to publication.

Finally, to you, the reader. Thank you for buying the book. I do hope you read it and I pray you talk about the hope we have as Christians with your family, friends, colleagues, and companions. To God be the glory, great things he has done!

Myk Habets
Doctor Serviens Ecclesiae
Auckland, New Zealand

Chapter 1

Introduction: An Inkling of What's to Come

This morning I have been trying to think about heaven, but without much success. I don't know why I should expect to have any idea of heaven. I could never have imagined this world if I hadn't spent almost eight decades walking around in it. People talk about how wonderful the world seems to children, and that's true enough. But children think they will grow into it and understand it, and I know very well that I will not, and would not if I had a dozen lives.[1]

REVEREND JOHN AMES, *GILEAD*

We do not want merely to see beauty, though, God knows, even that is bounty enough. We want something else which can hardly be put into words—to be united with the beauty we see, to pass into it, to receive it into ourselves, to bathe in it, to become part of it.[2]

C. S. LEWIS, "THE WEIGHT OF GLORY"

1. Robinson, *Gilead*, 77.
2. Lewis, "Weight of Glory," 106.

Do You Want to Go to Heaven?

Have you ever wanted to go to Heaven? I haven't always wanted to go there. Well, that is not quite correct. I have always wanted to go to Heaven but I have not always thought it would be a happy place to be. You see, converted as a child in a conservative church, I wanted to not go to Hell more than I wanted to go to Heaven, and so not going to Hell meant going to Heaven, and so I begrudgingly accepted that fact. In an age of flannelgraphs (ask your grandparents!) and monologues, my Sunday school teachers were faithful to a fault, but they lacked something—something I now find everywhere I look; they lacked a genuinely Christian imagination, and they did so, I think, because they had been victims of what someone has called "theological malpractice." What I "heard" when I was young is that Heaven is a place of the proverbial fluffy clouds, fat cherubs, church music (think 1970s—the age before even praise and worship music reached the hallowed shores of conservative Christianity), and inactivity. I now know that I was taught that we would be disembodied "souls" (whatever my teachers thought they were) resting in an eternal, pastel-colored, 1970s fundamentalist church home group; where the guests had forgotten it was a potluck dinner and so we just sat around having "feelloowship." As a young lad, that was as inspiring to me as a banquet of brussels sprouts! But I didn't want to go to Hell so Heaven was for me.

I am, of course, overplaying the actual reality of the situation, but only to make an important point: many of us have only known a caricature of Heaven. We have been short-changed and sold a half-truth as the whole truth. What if these images of Heaven are not real? What if the new heavens and the new earth are more real than our fleeting shadows of life here? What if what we experience here on earth in this lifetime is merely a foretaste of a much larger, more colorful, and more exciting life that awaits us in God's presence?

Forty years later we find a reversal of sorts in church thinking on the afterlife. If the Christian publishers are anything to go by, Heaven has made a comeback and is the place to be. The term *heavenly tourism* has been coined to refer to the accounts of those who claim to have been to Heaven and come back to tell us how good it is. I make no comment here about the truthfulness or otherwise of such accounts, I only observe the fact that this is happening.[3]

3. The confession of Alex Malarkey, who coauthored *The Boy Who Came Back from Heaven*, is one case in point. See http://www.washingtonpost.com/blogs/style-blog/

Colton Burpo's story is one such account. The account of Colton Burpo rocketed to the top of the New York Times Best Seller list and for a (short) season the movie version was incredibly popular.[4] Burpo's story is about a four-year-old boy who had a form of out-of-body experience and went to Heaven while on the operating table. Upon his "return," he tells of meeting Jesus, God the Father, and even the Holy Spirit in Heaven; not to mention relatives he had never before known, and a great host of people and animals all enjoying the presence of God. A pictorialized children's version of the story was also published and a website was established from which parents can download coloring sheets and other activities for children to learn the story for themselves.[5] With great hype, the book, the movie, and the paraphernalia came . . . and went. With motion picture blockbusters released in 2014 like *Noah* and *Exodus* to move on to, Colton and his story got left behind (yes that movie was re-released in 2014 as well!) for the next sensational thing.

I have read Colton's book (the big one) and enjoyed it, for the most part. Like all things of this nature, you have to read critically and use some biblical discernment, testing everything with Scripture so as not to perpetuate ideas that are not God-given. On the whole, I thought the story was reasonably consistent with God's description of the new heavens and the new earth in Holy Scripture. Having read the big book, I was happy to read the picture storybook with my two children (then ages five and seven), taking license at a few points to depart from the written text and add my own words that corrected Colton here and there, include a few added details Colton missed, and generally just edit the book based on what Holy Scripture tells us. My children enjoyed the story, asked *a lot* of questions, and it was one of those delightful teachable moments when, for a fleeting second, one thinks they may just have been a good parent. It was also the genesis of the idea for this book.

Parental Priesthood

Albert Einstein once observed that by the age of four children know more about the world from experience than they will ever be able to express no matter how smart they become. If that is anywhere near being true, and I

---

wp/2015/01/15/boy-who-came-back-from-heaven-going-back-to-publisher/.

4. Burpo and Vincent, *Heaven Is For Real*.

5. Burpo et al., *Heaven Is For Real for Kids*.

think it is, then it is during those formative years of childhood that parents have the greatest opportunity to pass on the content of their faith, both the facts and the feelings, as it were. But do we know enough to pass on? Have we searched the Scriptures ourselves, and become sufficiently acquainted with God's Word, to be the kind of teachers to our children they are so clearly created to require?

In Scripture the role of the priest is to represent people to God. The priest has duties to fulfill and a role to play in standing between God and his people and being a vehicle for communication and relationship. The role of the priest is essential to biblical Christianity. Of course, in the fullness of time our Lord and Savior Jesus Christ was sent to be our Great High Priest (Hebrews 4), our complete representative. Jesus' perfect priestly work does not render human priestly action redundant, though (1 Pet 2:9). What it does is relocate the work of the priest from the Jewish temple to the person of the incarnate Son himself. And so, united to Jesus Christ in faith, we are each given a priestly role—that of representing the people of God to the Father, in the Son, by the Holy Spirit. (Here I want you to know that I use this Trinitarian language for God throughout this book because the only God revealed to us is the triune God, and because we should learn how to relate to him more personally than we often do. Call this one of my hobbyhorses.)

What does that mean in terms of family life? Many things, for sure, but at least this: it is the job of Christian parents to represent their children until they come to saving faith in Jesus (and even after). We do this all the time when we act as legal guardians for our children. We sign our names on their behalf, we pay for their fees in their name, we make decisions for them until they can make them for themselves, and we often take onto ourselves the consequences of their actions until they can own them fully. In a sense, these are all priestly forms of ministry parents and caregivers offer to their children. But I want to say more than this and identify one key area of priestly ministry that parents and caregivers are called to, and that is the incredibly crucial role of naming God's presence for our children when they are not able to do this for themselves.

"When the Bible says God's voice is like thunder, is it really as loud as thunder?"

EMMA, AGE 5

Let me explain what I mean. My daughter wants to hear God—audibly and in real time. She wants to see God—with her eyes like she sees me each day. She wants to feel God—physically, like being able to give the Father a big hug. Until she can do that, she struggles to believe

4

God exists (and this as an eight-year-old). How to respond to that? Well, as a priest to my daughter, my job is to name the presence of God when she cannot. I believe God exists. I believe God is present. I believe God is more real than I am or you are. I feel God all the time. I see God all the time. I hear God all the time. And yet, I have never given God a physical hug, I have never seen God with my eyes, nor have I ever heard God audibly. I know of and have heard stories of other people who have. I have no comment here about that. The fact is, I haven't. And yet, God is closer to me than I am to myself. So how do I communicate this to my daughter? I name God's presence when she cannot.

Let me give you an example of how I respond to my daughter in this priestly way. My daughter loves to dance freely, to sing with reckless abandon, to draw, and to color. She loves beauty wherever it can be found: in music, creation, critters, and creatures. And so I say to my lovely little girl who desperately wants to see, hear, and feel God, "Who do you think created music? Music is God's idea. Where do you think your sense of music comes from? That feeling you get when you dance; that is the embrace of the Father. The way you get carried away when you sing; that is the voice of the Son. The way a smile beams across your face when you see a colorful butterfly or a clear rainbow; that is the Holy Spirit talking to you. God is all around you; God is near and far, present and distant, and loud and quiet. What do you mean you have never felt God or never seen God or never heard God? God is all around us—if you have the eyes to see and the ears to hear." And so I name the presence of God when she cannot. And there are other ways to do this was well, especially in the love we see shared between God's people. I point to the way my wife and I love each other and the love we have for our children as a way to see, hear, and feel God's presence (John 13:35), or I point to the way our faith community (at its best) is united in love (Matt 18:20). And so it goes.

With my son it is more about the joy he finds in sports and gymnastics, and in creating and building. Here I remind him that he is a created co-creator of God, an image of Christ with God-given capacities of invention and industry and physical ability. I tell him of the famous saying of Eric Liddell, the Christian Olympian and missionary, "God made me fast. And when I run, I feel His pleasure." It really doesn't matter what interests the child has, or what passions move them, there is always a link back to God because we are creatures and he is the loving Creator. And that is part of a parents' ministry of priesthood.

God is present in real and tangible ways, but it is a learnt skill seeing this. We learn this primarily through Holy Scripture of course. Scripture teaches us to name God's presence for where it is. Scripture is the voice of God speaking to us most clearly. And so, with my own children I try to continually point them to what God says in the Bible. There he tells them they are loved, they are accepted, they are cherished, they were created for a purpose, and that God loves them with a "never stopping, never giving up, unbreaking, always and forever love," as the wonderful *Jesus Storybook Bible* puts it.[6] In addition to Scripture, we then turn to works that faithfully seek to understand and apply the Bible to all areas of life. This book falls into that category.

"Is Heaven the place that God lives?"

RHYS, AGE 4

A Christian Imagination[7]

Understanding a parent's priestly role is important, and so too is having a Christian imagination. (I prefer to call it a baptized imagination, but my friends didn't think that term worked very well.) A Christian imagination is simply my way of expressing the fact that God invites his followers into a creative, dynamic, and even imaginative future when he offers us in Scripture glimpses into the future life we will enjoy. Why glimpses though? Why not an entire book on the afterlife or nothing at all? There is no definitive answer to that other than it was God's will, but we can offer a partial answer in addition to that. God speaks through Scripture in incomplete ways because he is inviting us into something that is far beyond our understanding. In that case, no amount of words could ever communicate the reality of the new heavens and the new earth. Conversely, providing no information about the afterlife would be strange, given the resurrection and ascension of Jesus. Jesus said that he was going to prepare a place for us (John 14:2), and so he tells us a little of this place we are going in order to inspire within us faith, hope, and love.

6. Lloyd-Jones, illustrated by Jago, *Jesus Storybook Bible*.

7. In the original draft of this book I used the phrase "baptized imagination," which I prefer; but feedback suggested the phrase was off-putting to many so I (reluctantly) changed it. If, like me, you are a bit of a rebel then please use the language of "baptized imagination" and keep the revolution alive! C. S. Lewis spoke of a "baptized imagination" in relation to his "conversion" experience in *Surprised by Joy*, 72, 168, 170.

I often hear from Christians (and many who should know better!) that we really can't know much about the afterlife so we may as well not talk about it. That is simply not true. There is a lot of information in Scripture on the new heavens and the new earth and my contention is that when we pay attention to what *is* there, something happens within us—a wild hope rises and our faith is enlarged, and we are inflamed with love. It is true, however, that we don't have an exhaustive knowledge of the afterlife, nor do we know as much as some Christians in print and on television might suggest we do, but we can know a lot more than most of us do presently.

What we have in Scripture is enough to get us started, and by *started* I mean we have enough to set our imaginations on fire. Now I want to be careful in how I am using the term *imagination*, and so I have prefixed it with the word *Christian*. Imagination without fact is simply fantasy. But fact without imagination is formulaic, or, dare I say, mathematical (I say this as one who never sat his higher college exams in mathematics, so forgive me). Christian beliefs (theology) are not an exercise in fantasy or mathematics, but are one of life and truth. And so theologians and storytellers need each other to connect the truth with life. Think of Jesus teaching in parables as a precedent. When it comes to the afterlife (what theologians call *eschatology* or the doctrine of last things) we need a Christian imagination more than ever. A Christian imagination is one in which the truths of Scripture fuel further thoughts after God and his revelation. As Martyn Lloyd-Jones described preaching, so we could equally describe good theology; it is "logic on fire."

There is something elusive about eschatology (to use that technical term for the end times). We know a certain amount as fact, and the following chapters will draw your attention to key biblical teaching we have on the new heavens and the new earth. But then what? What are we to do with this information? For my money, we are meant to talk about these things with one another and imagine, dream, inspire, and reflect upon what God has in store for us. With some education in the Scriptures we can have countless fruitful conversations with fellow saints—our children especially—about what we might be and do in the resurrection. Good storytelling (factually true stories or fairytales) involves making decisions about how much to tell the reader and how much to let the reader work things out for themselves.

Let me illustrate, even though I know this will upset some. I enjoy sci-fi movies (as I write this section I am wearing a Star Wars BB-8 shirt) and good sci-fi novels from time to time, but I am especially taken with the fantasy works of C. S. Lewis. In fact, I prefer Lewis's fantasies over those of his good friend J. R. R. Tolkien. *The Hobbit* I enjoyed, but found reading *The Lord of the Rings* takes too much time and has too much of the author explaining the minute details to me. When we compare their relative word counts we see that each volume of The Lord of the Rings series is approximately 150,000 words whilst each of Lewis's Chronicles of Narnia books is only approximately 48,000 words (this is also partly why I prefer Dostoevsky over Tolstoy). There is something about the sparseness of the Narnia books that is their genius. Lewis paints enough of a picture in the reader's mind for the reader to then take over, as it were, and fill in the gaps. Evelyn Underhill summarized this appeal in a sentence when she wrote, "It is this capacity for giving imaginative body to the fundamental doctrines of Christianity that seems to me one of the most remarkable things about your work."[8] Of course, filling in those gaps is a matter of subjective interpretation, despite the fact that one's imagination can be more or less correct. One can't claim, for instance, that their own vision of what Mr. Tumnus looks like is the definitive vision of what he *does* look like, but if you think Mr. Tumnus has wings then you are sorely mistaken. I hope you get the point. How God speaks of the afterlife in the Bible is a little like the way Lewis wrote his fantasies. There is enough there to paint a concrete picture, but there is nothing like a photograph or an encyclopedic entry. The very fact that within Scripture the biblical authors express their inability to completely portray what they were seeing is testament to this (Rev 1:15, etc.).

> "Is Heaven in space and do we just, like, float around?"
>
> EMMA, AGE 5

How to Use This Book

And so I come back to the point of my opening story: children (and the rest of us) have a created fascination with Heaven, God has spoken through his Word, and we have a priestly duty to pass on to our children (and others) what we have received. So what, and how, can we talk about Heaven in ways that are both faithful to Scripture and helpful for life? That is the focus of this short work. In what follows, I will raise a series of basic questions about the new heavens and the new earth. I will then endeavor to answer these questions in order to resource further (imaginative) conversations in this area. Many of the questions come from my own two children, and many

8. Underhill, *Letters of Evelyn Underhill*, 301.

other children I have had deliberate conversations with. The formal questions are of course mine, but throughout the book I will include the actual questions children have asked.

My source of knowledge throughout is Holy Scripture, so that will be our authoritative guide and I will start each chapter with some relevant teaching from the Bible. Unlike some other books with similar aims to mine, you won't read in these pages about sitting on fluffy white clouds, playing harps, looking at fat cherubs, and seeing Heaven as the realization of humanity's hopes and dreams, a utopia for good boys and girls.[9] Rather, the picture God has given us is more concrete, more physical, more colorful, and more exciting than that. I have called this section "Let's Listen." I have used a lot of Bible verses throughout what follows, sometimes including the full text, but for the sake of brevity I often just reference the biblical text. If you want to take this seriously, please read these texts as they are God's words to us, and they are the primary way God speaks his truth into our lives. (It is also a way of keeping me honest and making sure I am not making this stuff up.)

What we then find is what the church has discovered throughout her existence: hearing God speak in Scripture compels us to talk amongst ourselves and ask, after the disciples, "What does this mean?" As the Spirit guides us here, we add understanding to our faith and begin to think theologically, with the saints of history, about the new heavens and the new earth, and so a thinking section follows the Bible section. I have called this section "Let's Talk."

Theologically reflecting, in community, on God's Word, we are then (super)naturally led by the Spirit to work out our salvation with fear and trembling, to put our knowledge into action, and to use God's Word as a lamp to light our way. As such, the third section of each chapter will include my attempt to think through what this means for us in practice, as a family seeking to pass on to others what we have received and learnt together of God's ways and goodness. Academics call this applied theology but I have called this section "Let's Play."

From initial disinterest in Heaven I have now come full circle; the new heavens and the new earth fascinate me and instill me with hope. This is a doctrine that burns within me, as the disciples said to each other on the road to Emmaus, and it does so for one reason: Christ is in the middle of it. I have found, through reading Scripture, that we are not made for the world

---

9. For that kind of book you might (not) like to consider Shriver, *What's Heaven?*

as we know it but for the new heavens and the new earth, for the kingdom of God on earth, for God's manifest presence with us. And so it should be.

In the beginning God created the heavens and the earth, forming and filling his creation day by day, until the sixth day, the day when he made a creature different to the rest, a creature like himself—*adam*—male and female, in his image and likeness, and said of them, "It is very good" (Gen 1:31). And here, a collective question should go up to God from all human creatures: "Good for what?" The rest of Holy Scripture gives us the answer. "What are we very good for?" We are created to become more and more like Christ, to have a resurrected body like his, to live in the new heavens and earth with God the Father, Son, and Spirit, and to enjoy the renewed creation as he always intended it. Everything else we experience in life is merely the road along which we travel to this ultimate and blessed destination. And in the process we discover that our true home is not the one we currently know, but it is God's place, in God's presence, with God's people. Colossians 3:1–4 (New Living Translation) lays this out for us in stunning brevity.

> Since you have been raised to new life with Christ, set your sights on the realities of heaven, where Christ sits at God's right hand in the place of honor and power. Let heaven fill your thoughts. Do not think only about things down here on earth. For you died when Christ died, and your real life is hidden with Christ in God. And when Christ, who is your real life, is revealed to the whole world, you will share in all his glory.

It is the reality to which this passage speaks that I want my own children, and all God's children, to know and experience. With these words I invite you into the pages of this book and into what I hope will be a journey that, not unlike Lucy's wardrobe wanderings into Narnia, will be but an entrée into that feast which is even now being prepared for those who love God (Rev 19:7–10).

Summary

In this chapter I have tried to communicate the following:

- Heaven should be a place to which we look forward to going.
- We each have ideas about Heaven that are not biblical, so we have to unlearn some things.

- All we can reliably know about Heaven is what we are told in the Holy Bible.

- It is parents' job to acts as priests (godly representatives) to their children, naming God's presence when children can't.

- We know enough about life after death to have a confident trust in God, and enough to fuel some playful discussions about what life will be like then.

- This book is designed to be read and then to be discussed widely with family and friends.

Chapter 2

The Best of All Possible Worlds

(What is Heaven like?)

Boughton says he has more ideas about heaven every day. He said, "Mainly I just think about the splendours of the world and multiply by two. I'd multiply by ten or twelve if I had the energy. But two is much more than sufficient for my purposes."[1]

REVEREND JOHN AMES, IN *GILEAD*

There is no need to be worried by facetious people who try to make the Christian hope of "Heaven" ridiculous by saying they do not want "to spend eternity playing harps." The answer to such people is that if they cannot understand books written for grown-ups, they should not talk about them. All the scriptural imagery (harps, crowns, gold, etc.) is, of course, a merely symbolic attempt to express the inexpressible. Musical instruments are mentioned because for many people (not all) music is the thing known in the present life which most strongly suggests ecstasy and infinity. Crowns are mentioned to suggest the fact that those who are united with God in eternity share His splendor and power and joy. Gold is mentioned to suggest the timelessness of Heaven (gold does not rust) and the preciousness of it. People who take these symbols literally might as well

---

1. Robinson, *Gilead*, 173.

think that when Christ told us to be like doves, He means that we were to lay eggs.[2]

C. S. LEWIS, *MERE CHRISTIANITY*

What Heaven?

Ever wondered what Heaven is *really* like? What is Heaven like? That is the key question we all want an answer to. Fortunately, God has sought fit to provide us with pretty good insight into some key features of Heaven throughout the Scriptures, with a few notable high points in a few prominent texts. In this chapter we ask and answer this key question: What is Heaven like? Before we move into that, however, we have some housekeeping to do related to what we call this eternal home.

In normal everyday conversation we talk about Heaven in a variety of ways. Christians speak of Heaven as the place they go to when they die, as God's special dwelling place, and as our eternal home. Heaven is where God "lives." Angels come from Heaven, as does Jesus, and it is from Heaven that Jesus will be revealed (Matt 5:16, 45; 6:1, 9; 7:11; 18:14). (Those not committed to the Christian faith have their own *varied* ways of speaking about Heaven too, but we won't concern ourselves with that here.) When a believer dies they go to Heaven. But Heaven is not our final destination— Heaven is life after death, but it is not the eternal home of resurrected believers. Paul writes of the believers in Corinth that when they die they shall be absent from this body and present with the Lord (2 Cor 5:8). In a similar way our Lord himself assured the dying thief that he would be with him in Paradise "today" (Luke 23:43).

Heaven is technically Paradise, a Persian word picture for an outer garden, a pleasant waiting point, but it is not to be confused with the main house. Heaven is thus a dwelling place or a temporary lodging as a prelude to the resurrection and the new heavens and the new earth. Between death and final resurrection we are taught in Scripture that we will be conscious, alive, and well with Christ in the heavenlies (Luke 20:38). This is what we call Heaven or, more technically, Paradise. (The corresponding place for those outside of a saving relationship with Christ is called Hades.) Heaven/ Paradise, then, is a temporary abode, a place believers go to between their

2. Lewis, *Mere Christianity*, 137.

death on earth and their final resurrection (we call this the intermediate state). In this book I am almost always referring to our final state, and so I often use the language of "the new heavens and the new earth" to refer to that.

When we turn to Scripture to resource our beliefs about Heaven, we find this slightly more complex picture of our eternal home emerge. Reflecting this more complex picture, theologians (those Christians tasked with studying and interpreting the Scriptures on a full-time basis) don't speak of Heaven without qualification. Technically, there are two heavens (and two hells, but hey, this is complicated enough). Let me explain. Most of the New Testament teaching on Heaven concerns the time after Christ returns to earth to judge the living and the dead, after the resurrection of all people, and after God makes all things new. This is, specifically, what is called the new heavens and the new earth. This is God's design for all those who love him and faithfully worship him. This is the final state of those savingly united to Christ, full of the Spirit, and children of the Father. (The corresponding place for those outside of a saving relationship with Christ is called Hell/the Lake of Fire.)

Our ultimate destiny is to live in resurrected bodies in the new heavens and the new earth. This is the great hope of all Christians (John 5:28–29; 1 Cor 15:20–23; 2 Pet 3:13; Rev 21:1). The Old and New Testaments are consistent in their teaching on the new heavens and the new earth when, for instance, Isaiah prophesies, "For behold, I create new heavens and a new earth, and the former things shall not be remembered or come to mind" (Isa 65:17). Paul declares in Romans 8:19:

> For the creation waits in eager expectation for the children of God to be revealed. For the creation was subjected to frustration, not by its own choice, but by the will of the one who subjected it, in hope that the creation itself will be liberated from its bondage to decay and brought into the freedom and glory of the children of God. We know that the whole creation has been groaning as in the pains of childbirth right up to the present time. Not only so, but we ourselves, who have the firstfruits of the Spirit, groan inwardly as we wait eagerly for our adoption to sonship, the redemption of our bodies.

If Heaven technically refers to life after death, we might, with Tom Wright, refer to the new heavens and the new earth as "life after life after death."[3] It is an arresting phrase and that is what makes it so good, I think. The focus of this book is on life after life after death. I will often simply refer to this as "Heaven" for the sake of convenience, but that is not to be confused with the intermediate state.[4] In order to dispel notions of the new heavens and earth that are overly spiritual or otherworldly, I will use a variety of terms for the new heavens and the new earth derived from Scripture. Here I will speak of the renewed earth, or the kingdom of God, the city of God, Zion, or simply Heaven. In each case I am referring (unless otherwise made clear) to the new heavens and earth. Changing our language around Heaven will be an incredible gift to our children and could prove to be as significant as the content we go on to cover about what the new heavens and earth will be like.

With that little explanation out of the way we can move to a discussion of what Heaven (the new heavens and the new earth!) will be like as far as we can know from Scripture. While we can't know the "furniture of heaven" or the "temperature of hell," as Rienhold Niebuhr is credited with saying, Scripture is not silent.

Let's Listen

As the curtain of world history is drawn closed by God's judgment of the earth by the Lord Jesus Christ, eternity now enters into our reality as God makes all things new and ushers in the new heavens and the new earth. After the final judgment and the great resurrection, we look forward to entering into the promise of life eternal in all its joyous reality, in the presence of the triune God forever. We shall hear the voice of Jesus saying to us, "Come, O blessed of my Father, inherit the kingdom prepared for you from the foundation of the world" (Matt 25:34). We shall enter into the reality not only of a new world order but of a renewed world: new heavens and a new earth.

The first thing we want to affirm is that Heaven is a place. It may not be real estate we can identify on a star chart, but it is a place—a place unlike any we have ever encountered, but a place nonetheless. Jesus clearly

3. Wright, *Surprised by Hope*, 160.

4. If the issue of the intermediate state interests you enough you might like to read this rather technical essay on it: Habets, "Naked but Not Disembodied: A Case for Anthropological Duality."

said, "I go to prepare a place for you" (John 14:2–3). If Heaven were not a place, if it were non-spatial, it would simply be a sea of sentimentality, a shapeless void of self-imagination. The new heavens and new earth will be created by almighty God and it will exist. This new heavens and earth will be a kind of heaven-earth: Heaven will come down to earth and earth will be taken up into Heaven (Revelation 21). This signifies for us the fullness of joy and communion that will then exist between the triune God and us, and us with God, and God and us with all of creation. We know Heaven is a place because at Jesus' ascension he went somewhere and he wanted his disciples (that includes you and me) to know where he was going. "As they were looking on, he was lifted up, and a cloud took him out of their sight" (Acts 1:9). The angels witnessed to this and said, "This Jesus, who was taken up from you into heaven, will come in the same way as you saw him go into heaven" (Acts 1:11). One further line of evidence that convinces us that the new heavens and earth are a place is the fact of Jesus' bodily, physical resurrection, as the first fruits of our own bodily, physical resurrection. A human body has to occupy space and time, and so Jesus is somewhere and that somewhere is Heaven/Paradise and in the future will be the new heavens and earth. Jesus did say categorically before he departed earth that "when I go and prepare a place for you, I will come again and will take you to myself, that where I am you may be also" (John 14:3).

That Heaven is a place is clearly taught in Scripture. Where it is—that is another question altogether. We often speak of Heaven being up, up past the sky, and for good reason. In Scripture all heavenly traffic comes from above to below and goes back up again. In a gravitational reversal we might say, "What comes down must go up." But knowing that the earth is round, we know that Heaven can't literally be up, because what is up to one person is down to another; it depends where on earth you are standing. But the language and idea of going up is useful; it represents going somewhere else, going away; it clearly teaches that Heaven is a place. While Paul can say that Heaven in some sense begins now, just as if we were seated in heavenly places in Christ Jesus (Eph 2:6), it is literally correct to say that Heaven is a place we go to after death (and the new heavens and the new earth after the great resurrection; 2 Cor 5:8). Christ assured the disciples that he was going to prepare a place for them and that he would come again and take them to be with himself (John 14:3). The book of Hebrews urges us to look for that city which has foundations, whose maker and builder is God (Heb 11:10). And Peter writes of the inheritance, incorruptible and undefiled and unfading, that is reserved in Heaven for the Christian (1 Pet 1:4). Heaven is real and it is being prepared for those who love the Lord.

When thinking about Heaven and earth we have to operate out of quite a different set of assumptions than we normally do. Reading Scripture makes demands upon us that go beyond the ethical (things we should do). Our imaginations are stretched and we are asked to picture a different universe than the one we know. When Scripture speaks of Heaven and earth it is not asking us to think of Heaven as a planet within the universe—or just on the border of it. Heaven is not in our space-time continuum. It is no surprise that, as the folktale goes, Russian cosmonauts upon returning from space said, "We didn't find God up in space and so he doesn't exist."[5] If they had found a living room within which God was watching TV, I think we would have been genuinely shocked. Scripture invites us to think of Heaven and earth as two very different kinds of space, two very different kinds of matter, and involving two very different kinds of time.

> "Is there beer in Heaven?"
>
> GRANT, AGE 45

Heaven is a real place and as such the new heavens and earth will be a new cosmic reality. Behold, "I am making everything new!" (Rev 21:5). Revelation 21:23–26 tells us:

> The city does not need the sun or the moon to shine on it, for the glory of God gives it light, and the Lamb is its lamp. The nations will walk by its light, and the kings of the earth will bring their splendor into it. On no day will its gates ever be shut, for there will be no night there. The glory and honor of the nations will be brought into it.

Note here that one way of describing our new environment is as the New Jerusalem, the city of God on earth. And in that city there will be many mansions, prepared for those who love the Lord and have served him while alive on earth (John 14:2). Christ is right now preparing a place for us, preparing the city to receive its inhabitants, all the children of God.

In this new city, on the new earth, there will be no moon or sun there to provide light; God in Christ is all the light we require (Isa 60:19, 20; Rev 21:23–34). Here we are being asked to marvel and wonder at the fact that God's own splendor and majesty will illuminate our new home. No moon,

---

5. Reports say that Yuri Gagarin, the first man in space, uttered these words; however, no evidence for this has been found. Gagarin was thought to be a Russian Orthodox Christian, and as such he had already found God on earth!

no sun, and no church or temple will exist there, for God himself will be its temple (Rev 21:22). When we come to look at what we do in Heaven, we already know we won't be going to church (I hear the "amens" and "praise the Lords" from here). In the absence of a created light (moon and sun) we have the uncreated light of God's radiant presence. We have glimpses of this kind of thing in Scripture. We might recall Moses, who spent time with God on Mt. Sinai and when he came down his face was glowing—so much in fact that they had to put a bag over his head (Exod 34:29–35). Paul reflects on this after the giving of the Holy Spirit at Pentecost and declares in 2 Corinthians 3:7–18:

> Now if the ministry that brought death, which was engraved in letters on stone, came with glory, so that the Israelites could not look steadily at the face of Moses because of its glory, transitory though it was, will not the ministry of the Spirit be even more glorious? If the ministry that brought condemnation was glorious, how much more glorious is the ministry that brings righteousness! For what was glorious has no glory now in comparison with the surpassing glory. And if what was transitory came with glory, how much greater is the glory of that which lasts!
>
> Therefore, since we have such a hope, we are very bold. We are not like Moses, who would put a veil over his face to prevent the Israelites from seeing the end of what was passing away. But their minds were made dull, for to this day the same veil remains when the old covenant is read. It has not been removed, because only in Christ is it taken away. Even to this day when Moses is read, a veil covers their hearts. But whenever anyone turns to the Lord, the veil is taken away. Now the Lord is the Spirit, and where the Spirit of the Lord is, there is freedom. And we all, who with unveiled faces contemplate the Lord's glory, are being transformed into his image with ever-increasing glory, which comes from the Lord, who is the Spirit.

What a profound text! What is even more profound is that John of Patmos ups the ante, as it were, on Paul and says here that the greater glory we experience in the new covenant now as believers will be eclipsed by the yet greater glory of the Lord God who will dwell with us face to face in the new earth (Rev 22:4)! Jesus showed us a little of this glory when he was on earth in what we call the transfiguration (Luke 9:28–36). Both Paul and John had personally experienced this luminous splendor of God. Paul was blinded by the confrontation with Christ on the road to Damascus (Acts 9:1–9), and John was overwhelmed by the exalted Lord on the isle of

Patmos (Rev 1:12–17). These, however, are isolated accounts and are extremely rare. But in the new heavens and earth this will be the new normal for the children of God. To live in God's city on earth, the New Jerusalem, is to live in the continuous presence of the unveiled glory of the triune God.

So the new heavens and earth are a place, but what kind of place? If your upbringing mirrors mine to any extent you will immediately be thinking of the proverbial clouds, cherubs, perhaps harps, and other basically ethereal things. Well, we couldn't have been more wrong. The fact that there will be new heavens and a "new earth" (2 Pet 3:13; Rev 21:1) means that we will inhabit a physical creation, a renewed earth with all of its solidity, physicality, and . . . well, earthiness.[6] Romans 8:19–21 is one of the key texts that speaks about the renewal of creation, where Paul says,

> For the creation waits in eager expectation for the children of God to be revealed. For the creation was subjected to frustration, not by its own choice, but by the will of the one who subjected it, in hope that the creation itself will be liberated from its bondage to decay and brought into the freedom and glory of the children of God.

While we are speaking about the physical nature of the new heavens and earth we have to take note of the fact, already mentioned, that Jesus rose from the dead bodily, ascended into Heaven bodily, sits at the right hand of the throne of the Father bodily, and will return bodily. And his resurrection is the first fruits of our own future bodily resurrection. We shall populate the new heavens and the new earth with physical, human bodies. So we will live in a physical environment, in physical bodies. We will have more to say about this in the next chapter.

Scripture has more to say about the real, tangible, and physical nature of the new heavens and earth when it speaks of the fact that we shall eat and drink at the great marriage supper of the Lamb (Rev 19:9), that Jesus will drink wine again with his disciples in Heaven (Luke 22:18), that the "river of the water of life" will flow from "the throne of God and of the Lamb" through the "middle of the street" of the city (Rev 22:1), and that the "tree

---

6. Don't let the words "and there will be no sea" lead you into thinking in the new heavens and earth there will be no oceans, seas, lakes, and rivers. For the ancients, the sea was a source of chaos and evil, a symbolic representation of all that stands against God and his will. So here it is clearly used symbolically so that "no more sea" means "no more evil (people)." See Dan 7:3; Rev 13:1. So pack your togs (swimming outfit); I think you will need them!

of life" will bear "twelve crops of fruit, yielding its fruit every month" (Rev 22:2).

Modern physics (and I am no physicist!) tells us that you can't have space without time. That same reality applies to eternity. As spatial (physical) beings, we will be time-bound. So in the new heavens and earth there will be time, but not as we know it now. With no sun or moon, and so no night (Rev 21:25), it seems clear that we won't experience the tick-tock, twenty-four hour time we currently do (let's call that created time). But we will experience time as a succession of moments, in a linear fashion, one experience after another, after another. We won't be in a timeless void or sea of unconsciousness. Scripture is unanimous in speaking of the new heavens and new earth in time-bound ways when it speaks of activity there as a sequence of events (Rev 21:24–26; 22:2). Eternity is both a quality and a duration. In terms of duration, the bliss and joy of living with the triune God in the new heaven and earth will not end. In terms of quality, Jesus said, "Now this is eternal life: that they know you, the only true God, and Jesus Christ, whom you have sent" (John 17:3). Exactly how we will experience this new time (let's call it redeemed time) is beyond us, but it will be glorious, rich, abundant, and without end (Rev 21:4). As two American theologians, Lewis and Demarest, once said:

> Think of the most joy-filled moments in your life. Subtract the sadness that comes when we realize how fleeting our temporal pleasures are. Add the immediate presence of God. Multiple by infinity, and that yields something of what heaven will be like![7]

Heaven is a place, a physical environment, populated by resurrected humans who are also physical, and is time bound; but what is in Heaven? Here we turn to an incredibly rich passage of Scripture for guidance, Revelation 21–22. In short, the new heavens and earth are depicted in Scripture as a place of great beauty and endless joy, a place of perfect contentment, and blazing splendor. As the city of God, the kingdom of Heaven has "the glory of God, and its brilliance was like that of a very precious jewel, like a jasper, clear as crystal" (Rev 21:11). The new creation will be full of color, sights, sounds, and experiences. It will be a place of grandeur, beauty, and adventure. Images of Heaven

> "How will Heaven attach itself to the earth?"
>
> SYDNEY, AGE 9

---

7. Lewis and Demarest, *Integrative Theology*, 3:480

that use symbols like golden streets and pearly gates speak to this splendor and beauty (Rev 21:18–21). But more than this, the gold harkens back to the splendor of Solomon's temple (1 Kgs 6:20). Solomon's temple was a wonder of the ancient world, but it pales in comparison to the new heavens and earth. The twelve precious stones cemented into the walls of the New Jerusalem, the name of the city at the heart of the new earth, brings to mind Isaiah's prophecy of the coming kingdom of God adorned with precious stones, which speaks of the supreme worth of the place (Isa 54:11–12).

On our honeymoon my wife and I had the incredible opportunity to visit the Taj Mahal in India. What a sight of gleaming white marble, intricate tile art, and views out across the Yamuna River. It is remarkable. But, as our convivial tour guide constantly reminded us, this mausoleum was originally encrusted with "semi-precious stones and was a marvel of architecture and of art." What it must have looked like when it was first built by Shah Jahan! And all to honor his recently deceased wife Mumtaz Mahal. And yet the Taj Mahal is but a very pale comparison of the sort of picture John of Patmos paints for us from his revelation of the new earth to come. The precious stones adorning the new earth mentioned in Revelation allude to the twelve precious stones that festooned the ritual breast-plate (ephod) of the Jewish high priest and represented the twelve tribes of Israel (Exod 28:15–21). As the high priest carried the people of Israel with him into the presence of God, so in the new heavens and earth we are in the presence of the great High Priest, Jesus Christ, and as a visual reminder of his representation of us the stones remind us that we are enclosed about within the heart of God, "for whom each last individual is remembered and every person's concerns are his unceasing care."[8] What an exquisite picture of what is to come.

A final feature of what the new heavens and earth are like that I want to mention in this chapter is the most magnificent thing of all, the point of it all for John of Patmos, and the ultimate reason why we look so forward to going there. We are told that the new heavens and earth are God's dwelling place, the place where the Father, Son, and Holy Spirit dwell in unfettered majesty. In Revelation 21:3–4 we read:

> And I heard a loud voice from the throne saying, "Look! God's dwelling place is now among the people, and he will dwell with them. They will be his people, and God himself will be with them and be their God. 'He will wipe every tear from their eyes. There

8. Milne, *Message of Heaven and Hell*, 319.

will be no more death' or mourning or crying or pain, for the old order of things has passed away."

"God himself will be with us"! There is nothing more glorious or satisfying than that. God is with us now, of course, but then he will be with us in a more immediate way than he is even now by the Spirit. Then we will see him, feel him, talk with him, and commune with him in resurrected bodies that will, for the first time in our existence, be capable of being so close to God that we become more and more and more like him.

The triune God of grace and glory resides in the new heavens and the earth and he makes his home amongst us. "I saw the Holy City, the new Jerusalem, coming down out of heaven from God, prepared as a bride beautifully dressed for her husband" (Rev 21:2). God's home is now our home. No longer are we aliens and strangers in a strange land (1 Pet 2:11–12). Here we are home.

We have looked at every part of this text of Scripture already but it will pay us to read Revelation 22:1–5 in full:

> Then the angel showed me the river of the water of life, as clear as crystal, flowing from the throne of God and of the Lamb down the middle of the great street of the city. On each side of the river stood the tree of life, bearing twelve crops of fruit, yielding its fruit every month. And the leaves of the tree are for the healing of the nations. No longer will there be any curse. The throne of God and of the Lamb will be in the city, and his servants will serve him. *They will see his face, and his name will be on their foreheads.* There will be no more night. They will not need the light of a lamp or the light of the sun, for the Lord God will give them light. And they will reign for ever and ever.

Notice right there, at the heart of John's revelation, is the most glorious prospect awaiting believers: we shall see his face and we shall have his name displayed on our bodies. To face God and not be afraid will be a wondrous thing. To face God as one whose sins have not only been forgiven, but now forgotten, and without any possibility of sinning again—that will be heaven indeed. The invitation given in Hebrews 10:22 on the basis of Christ's sacrifice to "draw near to God" finds its fulfillment here. The psalmists long to see God's face (Pss 11:7; 27:4; 42:2) and the prophets of old could only dream of such a thing (Isa 52:8; 60:2; Zech 9:14). But one day, you and I, along with the psalmists and prophets, will experience what we now so long to have: the most intimate communion with God possible. Christian writer

Bruce Milne had a good illustration of the powerful hope we have of seeing God's face when he wrote:

> Helen Keller, after a lifetime of blindness, was once asked what she would do if, for just one day, the power of sight were restored to her. She replied, "I should call to me all my dear friends and look long into their faces." What a prospect for every child of God, to be called into the presence of the dearest Friends of our lives, whom we have here known by faith and not by sight, and there to look, and look, for ever.[9]

But what of this concept of being branded on our foreheads with God's name? This branding is a seal of ownership and is not to be taken literally, as if we will each have a tattoo on our foreheads. It speaks to the fact that we are God's; he owns us, he has purchased us with the life and death and resurrection of Jesus Christ and with the sending of the Spirit (2 Cor 1:22; 5:5; Eph 1:4), and we are his forever. This seal in Revelation 22:4 is the opposite of the seal "666" given to those who follow the antichrist (Rev 13:16–17). The seal identifies us as belonging to God. What we find here is the ultimate fulfillment of promises God has been making to us since the beginning. We are especially reminded of the Aaronic benediction in Numbers 6:22–26, which reads:

> The Lord said to Moses, "Tell Aaron and his sons, 'This is how you are to bless the Israelites. Say to them:
> "'The Lord bless you and keep you;
> the Lord make his face shine on you and be gracious to you;
> the Lord turn his face toward you and give you peace.'"

The benediction concludes with verse 27: "So they will put my name on the Israelites, and I will bless them." What has been partial and incomplete throughout the history of the world will now be fulfilled; we shall see God and be his people forever.

We could add more details to our description of what the new heavens and earth will be like. We could talk about the walls of the city of God (200 feet thick) and how they speak of an eternal security experienced at that time where God is our protector (Rev 21:12–14). We could talk about the size of the city (1,400 miles wide, long, and high), a perfect cube of enormous size (Rev 21:15–17), a highly symbolic representation of the new earth that alludes to the proportions of the holy of holies in the temple in

9. Ibid., 325.

Jerusalem (1 Kgs 6:22). There is no temple in the new earth because it is all a temple: "I did not see a temple in the city, because the Lord God Almighty and the Lamb are its temple" (Rev 21:22). The entire environment is the holy of holies within which the presence of God dwells most fully to bless. The work fulfilled by Christ in his death (Matt 27:51) now comes to complete fruition. Our new home will be in the presence of the all-holy God. Enough has been said, though, for us to get an accurate picture of what the new heavens and earth will be like: a place, physical, time-bound, glorious, bright, safe, colorful, expansive, intimate, communal, and all this in the presence of the Father, Son, and Holy Spirit. Now what to make of all this.

Let's Talk

In this section we move from observing what the Bible says to interpreting what it means when we put it all together. When we synthesize the biblical information, and bring in other truth God has revealed to us, we formulate what we call doctrines; fundamental beliefs derived from God's revelation. So what can we say about what the new heavens and earth will be like? Five essential features of what the new heavens and earth will be like have been briefly examined above: (1) it is a place; (2) it occupies redeemed space and time; (3) it is a city with many mansions, safe walls, dazzling brilliance, and bewildering size; (4) it is the dwelling place of the triune God whose splendor fills the city, providing light, safety, belonging, and intimacy; and (5) it is a physical environment with trees, fountains, buildings, food, drink, colors, sights, smells, and sounds. But those are the bare facts; the blueprint, if you like, of what our eternal home will be like.

What theologians do with all this information is pray through it, read what the saints of history have said about this, talk to fellow believers in church, and reflect deeply on what God has said, and then attempt to write a summary or a synthesis of all this, aimed at teaching and training Christians into a mature faith, at guarding and defending believers from false views which might lead them astray, and constructing a compelling and faithful account of what God has said in the language of the day. When we come to the new heavens and the new earth, theologians put this under the category of *eschatology*, a word derived from the Greek language of Jesus' day that simply means a doctrine of things to come. And that is what you and I are doing as parents to our children; we are their theologians, teaching, correcting, and discipling them to think thoughts after God. On the basis of what we have heard from God's Word, how might we now talk of the new heavens and the new earth?

The new heavens and the new earth represent the final restoration of Israel and the church, united in their faith to Jesus Christ. The New Jerusalem, the city of God, is ruled by Christ, and is impenetrable with its position atop an enormous hill, with its ridiculously thick walls, and with its twelve foundations and twelve gates protected at all times by twelve angels. But it is a city like no other. Its twelve gates are always open, welcoming believers into its precincts. It has no temple or church buildings, for the entire city (earth) is the Lord's dwelling place. As such, we can say the joining together of Heaven and earth in union with Christ has always been God's goal for the universe and the creatures within it, and that is why it is the final destination of God's people (Eph 1:10).

In this renewed creation we will enjoy all the physical realities we do here on earth, but in unfettered ways, in the absence of the frustrating and despoiling consequences of sin and the fall, and in the presence of God himself—the Father to worship, Christ as our guide, and the Spirit to perfect and equip (amongst multiple other activities God does all the time). Australian theologian Michael Bird summarizes a theology of the new heavens and earth this way:

> The final state is a heaven that descends to earth and an earth that receives the heavens, so that both heaven and earth are transformed into something other than what they were before. Heaven and earth are changed into the new creation. Heaven does not swallow up earth and earth does not simply absorb heaven. The earth is transfigured and transformed into a heavenly plane of existence, and the dividing line between heaven and earth is obliterated. Heaven becomes earthly and earth becomes heavenly. Though heaven is life after death, the new creation is life after life after death. [10]

It is not hard to spot the influence of N. T. Wright on Bird's language, and it is interesting how he picks up on the uniting of Heaven and earth in the new creation. In the same vein, Bruce Milne reminds us that "Heaven is not so much a new world 'up there' as a new world 'down here.'"[11]

---

10. Bird, *Evangelical Theology*, 328.

11. Milne, *Message of Heaven and Hell*, 310.

Another issue that we are confronted with is working out whether the new earth will be a brand new one after this present one is annihilated, or will be a renewed earth. On biblical and theological grounds too vast to track here, I favor the view that this present world will be renewed when Christ comes again.[12] This renewal is radical and mind-blowing, such that it can only be described in what we call apocalyptic language (2 Pet 3:12–13), as "passing away" (Rev 21:2–3). But, along with many, I see this as a reference to the end of creation in its current state and form—fallen and estranged from God, suffering decay and entropy. Just as humans are not annihilated but resurrected, so too the cosmos itself will undergo a form of resurrection and thus be both continuous with what we know of the earth now and in some sense discontinuous. What 2 Peter 3 refers to is not the destruction of the earth but the complete transition of the cosmic order from fallen to redeemed (Rom 8:18–26).

This has implications for us today. Some forms of Christianity looked to the coming of the Lord as the end of this world and the creation of a brand new one. When they applied this teaching, the net effect was to teach that we should suck this world dry of all its natural resources as quickly as possible, maximize land production to its greatest capacity (and beyond), and exploit nature purely for human enjoyment and rising living standards. In short, the attitude was that we only have this world for a short time so let's make sure we use it all up. This has resulted in unsustainable farming practices, radical pollution, systemic poverty, and an exploitation of the poor and marginalized. Michael Horton helpfully paints the contrast with what Scripture teaches us about a renewed heavens and earth:

> If our goal is to be liberated *from* creation rather than the liberation *of* creation, we will understandably display little concern for the world that God has made. If, however, we are looking forward to the "restoration of all things" (Acts 3.21) and the participation of the whole creation in our redemption (Rom 8.18-21), then our actions here and now pertain to the same world that will one day be finally and fully renewed.[13]

What we have to look forward to in the new heavens and the new earth is a world in which there is perfect balance, perfect peace, and perfect relations between creatures and the creation. We regularly read about this

12. For a summary of the arguments in favor of this position see Peterson, "Pictures of Heaven," 164.

13. Horton, *Christian Faith*, 989–90.

town in Kansas being wiped out by a hurricane, or that city being swept away by a tsunami, or this county being devastated by an earthquake. As I write this chapter, Christchurch, a city in my own country of New Zealand, has just experienced another major earthquake. Five years ago two massive quakes hit (in 2010 and 2011), killing over 185 people, collapsing cliffs, destroying buildings, and swallowing property and with it people's sense of security and stability. The new heavens and the new earth will have no such so-called "acts of God." Instead, God will maintain what he has made, keeping sin and its devastatingly chaotic consequences out.

We can look forward to sustainable development, bountiful crops, produce for all, healthy ecosystems, abundant life, clean water, no GE food, and grapes so good the wine is literally out of this world. No one knows the number of species that have gone extinct but WWF estimates there may be 100 million different species on earth, and if the extinction rate is just 0.01 percent a year then at least 10,000 species go extinct each year! Imagine a world in which there is no extinction, in which these 100 million species flourish. Imagine also a redeemed earth in which God *may* (we don't know for certain) bring extinct species back into existence. God created creatures with a spoken word in the first place and it is not too much to think he might bring back entire species that have become extinct. Then we are asked to imagine a world with more variety, abundance, color, sounds, smells, and sights than we can currently imagine—a world so diverse and magnificent, in fact, that we would need new eyes to see it all, new minds to apprehend it all, and new imaginations to care for and steward such a place. And God has that covered by giving us resurrected bodies.

Considering the stereotypes of Heaven that we have inherited—the proverbial clouds and harps, cherubs and church music—we should more naturally associate the new heavens and earth with an Indian wedding celebration, where there is more color, food, music, and dancing on display than the senses can bear. I have seen Indian weddings with painted elephants and outdoor marquees of a thousand hues, celebrations extending for days, and smiles etched across people's faces. That is more like a picture of Heaven that corresponds to the biblical vision. Or perhaps we could think of an Amazonian jungle, minus the lethal tendencies of many of its animal and vegetable residents—a jungle thick and lush, screaming out to be explored, photographed, and enjoyed. Or we could think of a great South African safari park, with the safety of the guides, but amidst the majestic wild of the big cats and water beasts. Or perhaps we could think of the music hall or a gig. That, at least, is how children's folk group Butterflyfish portray it in their song "Music," a delightful and creative take on the new heavens and earth. They sing (and my daughter sings along with them at full voice, and has done so for over five years now):

> (Chorus) We are going, to a place where music, falls and fills up everything. Though it might be a long time, we know it's gonna be alright, 'cause we've already started to sing.
>
> Come and go with me, we can walk together, climb any mountain, brave any weather. That place we're going, is a beautiful song. While we're on our way we can sing along.
>
> (Chorus)
>
> And when we get there, and join that choir, everybody's gonna be there, a world on fire. And the light will shine, on that endless day. We can sing through the night while we're on our way."
>
> (Chorus)[14]

How good is that to provoke conversation and to represent just something of what our real destiny holds out for us? If you want an alternative to music, you could work with the category of beauty (aesthetics, as the know-it-alls call it). C. S. Lewis touched on this when he penned the following: "We want something else which can hardly be put into words—to be united with the beauty we see, to pass into it, to receive it into ourselves, to bathe in it, to become part of it."[15] As with music so with beauty, art, and other creative activities; we long to connect, to touch, to experience, and to "enter into" these moments, the music, the vision, the dance. The new heavens and the new earth actually make this happen, as we enter into joy eternal.

When our children think of what awaits them in the new heavens and the new earth, and we walk them through the biblical vision of what is to come, watch their eyes widen, their minds tick over, and their faces beam with excitement. And then hold on to the kitchen table as an avalanche of questions, what-ifs, and wild excitement takes over. And if you listen carefully at such moments, you may indeed hear God smile. According to Randy Alcorn,

> When we hear that in Heaven we will have new bodies and live on a New Earth, this is how we should understand the word *new*— a restored and perfected version of our familiar bodies and our

14. Butterflyfish, "Music," *Ladybug* (Matthew Boulton, 2009).
15. Lewis, "Weight of Glory," 107.

familiar Earth and our familiar relationships. Because we once lived on Earth, the New Earth will strike us as very familiar.[16]

Tom (N. T.) Wright always has a wonderful way of summarizing deep truths in simple but accurate ways. When examining the new heavens and earth he concludes, "The new world will be more real, more physically solid, than the present one . . . We speak of people being 'shadows of their former selves'; if 2 Corinthians 5.1–10 is correct, we should think of ourselves as being shadows of our future selves in God's purpose."[17] We could say the same for the current heavens and earth being shadows of their future forms as well. No one has made more profound use of this concept of the new earth being more real, more physical, and more "earthy" than C. S. Lewis in his masterful allegory *The Great Divorce*. The central theme of this work is an idea summarized in another of his works, namely, that "It is the present life which is the diminution, the symbol, the etiolated, the (as it were) 'vegetarian' substitute. If flesh and blood cannot inherit the Kingdom, that is not because they are too solid, too gross, too distinct, too 'illustrious with being'. They are too flimsy, too transitory, too phantasmal."[18] Here is an idea worth wrestling with at length.

Let's Play

It would be a useful exercise to "play" with a number of these concepts with your children; to explore the tension between feeling the pull or allure of Heaven and the fact that it is still to come, the sheer size of the place and what that might mean for living there, the grandeur and splendor of living with the triune God, the incredible abundance of life there, and the fact that it is life eternal. Knowing what beliefs, feelings, and environment is presented in biblical portrayals of Heaven all helps to "dream," "imagine," and begin to value God's home which is being made ready for us. My goal is that by working through the first two sections of this chapter I can keep this final section brief, as you will now be able to formulate your own questions, ideas, and teachable moments with your children around this topic. What follows is simply a teaser for your own ideas of how to play with these biblical concepts.

16. Alcorn, *Heaven*, 50.

17. Wright, *New Heavens, New Earth*, 12.

18. Lewis, "Transposition," 90.

In the final book of the Chronicles of Narnia, *The Last Battle*, C. S. Lewis has Aslan (the Christ figure) bring some of the Pevensey children and their family from the Shadowlands (the "old" Narnia) into the land of the Emperor over the sea (God the Father's home in the new heavens and earth). As he does, the following conversation (one of the best in all the works of fiction!) is recorded in which Lucy, the youngest and most faithful of the children, reflects on how the new earth looks much like the old earth, and yet different.

"Those hills," said Lucy, "the nice woody ones and the blue ones behind—aren't they very like the southern border of Narnia."

"Like!" cried Edmund after a moment's silence. "Why they're exactly like. Look, there's Mount Pire with his forked head, and there's the pass into Archenland and everything!"

"And yet they're not like," said Lucy. "They're different. They have more colours on them and they look further away than I remembered and they're more . . . more . . . oh, I don't know . . . ."

"More like the real thing," said the Lord Digory softly.

Suddenly Farsight the Eagle spread his wings, soared thirty or forty feet up into the air, circles round and then alighted on the ground.

"Kings and Queens," he cried, "we have all been blind. We are only beginning to see where we are. From up there I have seen it all—Ettinsmuir, Beaversdam, the Great River, and Cair Paravel still shining on the edge of the Eastern Sea. Narnia is not dead. This is Narnia."

"But how can it be?" said Peter. "For Aslan told us older ones that we should never return to Narnia, and here we are."

"Yes," said Eustace. "And we saw it all destroyed and the sun put out."

"And it's all so different," said Lucy.

"The Eagle is right," said the Lord Digory. "Listen, Peter. When Aslan said you could never go back to Narnia, he meant the Narnia you were thinking of. But that was not the real Narnia. That had a beginning and an end. It was only a shadow or a copy of the real Narnia, which has always been here and always will be here: just as our own world, England and all, is only a shadow or copy of something in Aslan's real world. You need not mourn over Narnia, Lucy. All of the old Narnia that mattered, all the dear creatures, have been drawn into the real Narnia through the Door. And of course it is different; as different as a real thing is from a shadow or as waking life is from a dream." . . .

The difference between the old Narnia and the new Narnia was like that. The new one was a deeper country: every rock and flower and blade of grass looked as if it meant more. I can't describe it any better than that: if you ever get there, you will know what I mean.

It was the Unicorn who summed up what everyone was feeling. He stamped his right forehoof on the ground and neighed and then cried:

"I have come home at last! This is my real country! I belong here. This is the land I have been looking for all my life, though I never knew it till now. The reason why we loved the old Narnia is that is sometimes looked a little like this."[19]

Here is a piece of my own Christian imagination. With the new heavens and earth there will be an entire universe to explore. Who knows, but it is not out of the question that this universe will be expanding, just like our one now (Isa 9:7 could be relevant here). And on our planet we know there is such fecundity, might there be so on other planets? This is part of the human quest for space travel now. Might it be possible that in eternity we will be able to travel through space, either in rockets we have built or through some form of space travel? It is speculation but not *wildly* so. We have seen that Heaven is as much a dimension in God's time as it is a place, and so inhabiting such a place could mean space exploration is on the cards. I certainly hope so. But if space is not your thing, then what about exploring the depths of the ocean floor, getting "lost" in a rainforest, or lying on your back watching the sky as something like the Aurora Borealis on a larger expanse dances above us, and all with a cup of cocoa and fine company? What do your children like to do? What do they want to do? How might the new heavens and the new earth afford them opportunities to do these things? You might like to have a competition to see who can come up with the most unusual thing to do there. Or the most enjoyable thing. Or the loudest thing. Or the quietest. Or you might like to name the five senses (sight, hearing, taste, smell, and touch) and try to identify or imagine one thing in the new heavens and earth that might correspond to each.

> "When you die and go to Heaven, do you turn into a skeleton?"
>
> Emma, age 5

One way to discuss some of this around the dinner table or in children's church is to ask kids to discuss the claim that "the city of Heaven

19. Lewis, *Last Battle*, 168–71 (Collier).

is better than the garden of Eden." Tease out of them what the creation story tells us about how God created the world in order, with beauty, with abundance, and created two people—Adam and Eve—to tend and steward creation. You might like to play up how good this all is, how lovely and peaceful it is (or at least was, before sin ravished it all). Then throw them the curve ball: "But the new heavens and earth will be better than that!" And it will be. I hope you are now in a position to begin to discuss with children how it will be better. If you want some help in this area I cannot recommend more highly for adults the Cosmic Trilogy by C. S. Lewis, especially the second book, *Perelandra. Perelandra* is one of those rare books that can transform our vision and offer a fictitious but profoundly helpful picture of what a redeemed and renewed earth could look like. In the final chapter Lewis manages to combine a whole series of biblical images and themes together into a scene dripping with imaginative insights into what might be on the new earth. Speaking about this book, Wayne Martindale sums up my own reading experience when he writes:

> Upon arriving in the new world, Ransom [the lead human character] revels in a landscape of unspeakable beauty and hospitality to him as a human. He floats on the oceans, finding the water refreshing to drink; enjoys the help of the animals, who delight in aiding him; is dazzled by its colors, including a sky that suggests the aurora borealis; and discovers a new genus of pleasure in the tastes of its fruits and the refreshing baths of the bubble trees that burst over him with a kind of super Gatorade invigoration, Perelandra's human-like couple, the Adam and Eve of this new world, are in harmony with nature, both flora and fauna, and are in easy, regular communion with God. In no other reading experience have I felt so keenly, so imaginatively, the price in our world exacted by sin. And more than any other book, it suggests to my imagination how marvellous the re-creation of our own world will be when God restores the harmony shattered by disobedience.[20]

"Since we have a new body in Heaven, do we still have a face?"

RILEY, AGE 4

When children think about the new heavens and earth they have lots of questions. These are some that I have heard (and solicited).

"Can you get to Heaven in a rocket ship?" The question assumes the new heavens and earth exist in our time and space. We know

20. Martindale, *Beyond the Shadowlands*, 69.

now that they don't. So no, you can't get there in a rocket ship. But in Christ, Heaven is only a heart's breath away.

"Can you time travel in Heaven?" The question asks if time and space will be the same as they are now, and we already know they are not. So can we time travel? Well, immediately above I was questioning our ability to space travel, so perhaps time traveling is not out of the question. But we know we won't be able to travel *back* in time, for the old heavens and the old earth have passed away (Rev 21:1). And what would it mean to travel into the future of eternity, where a day is like a thousand years and a thousand years are like a day? (2 Pet 3:8). But traveling through time in eternity may involve more options than back and forward only. That is something for our theoretical physicist friends to ponder.

As this chapter comes to a close I want to make explicit the key emphasis I have attempted to bring out in relation to what the new heavens and earth will be like; namely, the physicality of it all and the centrality of God: Father, Son, and Holy Spirit. We need to unlearn the (false) teaching that Heaven (in its intermediate state and in its final state) is an ethereal, "spiritual" (if by spiritual we mean not physical), and mystical (if by mystical we really mean weird) place inhabited by ghosts and furnished with ghostly architecture. That is simply not what God has taught us in Holy Scripture.

As American Pastor John Piper reflects on God's wondrous creation, and the more wondrous Creator of it all, he recalls a lecture given by Clyde Kilby in 1976, where he resolved to "sometimes look back at the freshness of vision I had in childhood and try, at least for a little while, to be, in the words of Lewis Carroll, the 'child of the pure unclouded brow, and dreaming eyes of wonder.'" Reflecting on that resolution, Piper concludes:

> One of the tragedies of growing up is that we get used to things. It has its good side of course, since irritations may cease to be irritations. But there is immense loss when we get used to the redness of the rising sun, and the roundness of the moon, and the whiteness of the snow, the wetness of rain, the blueness of the sky, the buzzing of bumble bees, the stitching of crickets, the invisibility of wind, the unconscious constancy of heart and diaphragm, the weirdness of noses and ears, the number of the grains of sand on a thousand beaches, the never-ceasing crash crash crash of countless waves, and ten million kingly-clad flowers flourishing and withering in woods and mountain valleys where no one sees but God.

Piper then offers an invitation based on these reflections, one which I too would share with you.

> I invite you, with Clyde Kilby, to seek a "freshness of vision," to look, as though it were the first time, not at the empty product of accumulated millennia of aimless evolutionary accidents (which no child ever dreamed of), but at the personal handiwork of an infinitely strong, creative, and exuberant Artist who made the earth and the sea and everything in them. I invite you to believe (like the children believe) "that today, this very day, some stroke is being added to the cosmic canvas that in due course you shall understand with joy as a stroke made by the Architect who calls Himself Alpha and Omega."[21]

The next generation of Christians needs to grow up knowing and believing that the new heavens and earth will be more physical than what we currently know, full of glory, majesty, color, and on fire with adventure; a place of delight because God dwells there in unbounded glory and intimacy. In the next chapter we examine what we will be like in Heaven and what on earth we will do there.

Summary

In this chapter I have tried to communicate the following:

- Scripture speaks of three *heavens*: 1) the atmosphere above us, 2) outer space, and 3) God's abode.

- When Christians use the word *heaven* they often mean our final destination.

- Holy Scripture never speaks of Heaven as our final destination.

- Technically, Heaven is the abode of God where believers go between death and final resurrection.

- According to Scripture, the final destination for believers will be the new heavens and new earth.

- When talking about our final destination we might speak of this as "life after life after death."

- The new heavens and earth are a place and not just a state.

21. Piper, *Pleasures of God*, 96

- The new heavens and earth have their own time, space, and environment.

- The new creation will be full of color, sights, sounds, and experiences.

- The triune God of grace and glory resides in the new heavens and the earth and he makes his home amongst us.

- The earth will be renewed, not replaced.

- The new world will be more real, more physically solid, than the present one.

- The new heavens and earth are more exciting than many of us have been led to believe.

- So, do you want to go there?

Chapter 3

Raised Immortal

(What Will We Be Like in the Resurrection?)

"Ah, Ruth! a bliss beyond speech is waiting us in the presence of the Master, where, seeing Him as He is, we shall grow like Him, and be no more either dwarfed or sickly. But you will have the same face, Ruth, else I should be for ever missing something."

"But you do not think we shall be perfect all at once?"

"No, not all at once; I cannot believe that: God takes time to do what he does—the doing of it is itself good . . ."

They were walking like children, hand in hand: Ruth pressed that of her uncle, for she could not answer in words.[22]

POLWARTH, *PAUL FABER, SURGEON*

It is a serious thing to live in a society of possible gods and goddesses, to remember that the dullest and most uninteresting person you talk to may one day be a creature which, if you saw it now, you would be strongly tempted to worship. . . . There are no ordinary people. You have never talked to a mere mortal. . . . But it is immortals whom we joke with, work with, marry, snub, and exploit—immortal horrors or everlasting splendours.[23]

C. S. LEWIS, "THE WEIGHT OF GLORY"

22. MacDonald, *Paul Faber, Surgeon* (1878), ch. 51.
23. Lewis, "Weight of Glory," 109.

A belief in the afterlife is one thing; knowing what to believe in is quite another. In the previous chapter we looked at what the new heavens and earth will be like, taking particular notice of the physical nature of God's renewed universe and the centrality of the triune God to our new existence. In this chapter we examine a question we have all asked at one time or another, and our kids ask us when they are at their theologically deepest: what will *we* be like in the resurrection? The Bible is very clear when it comes to what we will be like and it paints some fascinating and exciting pictures of what we will do there. This chapter only begins to explore some of the first question, what we will be like, while the next chapter explores what we will do there; even though there will be some necessary overlap.

Let's Listen

A central feature governing what we will be like in the new heavens and earth is the resurrection. What was distorted and destroyed by the fall at creation will be reversed by the resurrection at the renewed creation. Paul states in 1 Corinthians 15:22 that "as in Adam all die, so in Christ all will be made alive." At the Parousia—the second coming of Christ—all shall be resurrected and made alive, some to be with Christ forever, others to live outside the city in what the Bible calls Hell (John 5:28). The resurrection is so important for how we are to understand what we will be like in Heaven that the New Testament spends a good deal of time talking about this. One text in particular stands center stage—1 Corinthians 15. It will pay us to look at this text closely (and a few others along the way) in order to gain our bearings for a discussion on what we will be like in Heaven.

The first thing we want to affirm is the fact of a future *bodily* resurrection. Jesus taught us, "But about the resurrection of the dead—have you not read what God said to you, 'I am the God of Abraham, the God of Isaac, and the God of Jacob'? He is not the God of the dead but of the living" (Matt 22:32). As sure as God is God, we shall be raised to new life. Paul teaches the same thing in Philippians 3:21, where we learn that we eagerly await a Savior from Heaven who will "transform our lowly bodies so that they will be like his glorious body." Here Paul contrasts our present bodies as lowly with Christ's glorious resurrected body. Our bodies are lowly here because they are temporary, ravaged by sin, and affected by the fall. Currently our bodies are wasting away, are prone to viruses, and are weak. Then, says Paul, our bodies will be what God always intended them to be: healthy, strong, fit, and capable of imaging God in Christ in, well, glorious ways.

At this point we have to make clear one of the myths that the resurrection shatters: that of the immortality of the soul. This is an ancient Greek idea, not a Christian one. At the resurrection the gift of eternal life (immortality) is given to us, as we receive bodies like Christ's (1 Cor 15:12–19). Both baptism and Communion (the Lord's Supper, or Eucharist) proclaim the reality of the resurrection. If you think about it, we are baptized bodily and we physically eat and drink the bread and wine; both acts being foretastes and parables of the embodied life to come in the resurrection. The resurrection is to immortality (life everlasting) in an embodied existence; it does not speak of a disembodied soul drifting through space.

According to 1 Corinthians 15:49, at the return of Christ believers will be raised up to receive new bodies, after the pattern of the resurrection body of Jesus Christ. This integral link between the resurrection of Jesus Christ and our own future resurrection, and the way that Christ's rising from the dead is foundational for our own future life (1 Cor 15:14), is foundational for Paul. Paul is clear about the order of things: first Christ is risen (1 Cor 15:3–4, 23), then follows a spiritual resurrection for believers (Eph 2:1–6; Rom 6), followed eventually by our physical resurrection (1 Cor 15:23).

We also see a teaching that has troubled people for a long time, but need not: "it is sown a natural body, it is raised a spiritual body. If there is a natural body, there is also a spiritual body" (1 Cor 15:44). The contrast here is not one between a physical and a non-physical body. Paul is also not thinking here of some dualism between bodies/physical and spirits/ non-physical. What Paul is saying is that there is a difference between our bodies here and our bodies there. In their present form our physical bodies simply cannot withstand the withering presence of the almighty God. We have no capacity to endure his blinding splendor, to hear his majestic voice, or to apprehend his lovely countenance. We can neither see God nor hear God without a veil existing between us. In short, says Paul, "flesh and blood cannot inherit the kingdom of God" (1 Cor 15:50). In order to participate fully in the new heavens and earth, to see God face to face, and to live in his presence, we must be glorified, resurrected, and changed into the likeness of Christ. "Flesh and blood in its present fallen condition simply cannot endure the joys of Zion."[24]

The good news is, our bodies will be changed (1 Cor 15:51), but not replaced. In the resurrection we are given immortality and imperishability (1 Cor 15:52–53). We shall be like Christ (Rom 8:11; Phil 3:21). The

24. Horton, *Christian Faith*, 916.

contrast Paul speaks about here is not between our present physical body and some future non-physical body, but a contrast between this body in its fallen state and its future glorious condition like that of Christ's own body. The word *spiritual* in 1 Corinthians15:44 is an adjective describing *body*; it is not arguing against having a body. Paul did not say and did not mean "it is sown a natural body, it is raised a spirit." According to Randy Alcorn—and I have no reason to disagree with his interpretation here—"Judging from Christ's resurrection body, a spiritual body appears most of the time to look and act like a regular physical body, with the exception that it may have (and in Christ's case it *does* have) some powers of a metaphysical nature; that is, beyond normal physical abilities."[25] It would be clearer, then, to speak of *renewed* bodies as opposed to new bodies.

A fundamental feature of the biblical teaching about what we will be like in the resurrection is that there will be both continuity and discontinuity between our bodies now and our bodies then. Knowing where to put the stress on both the continuity and the discontinuity is the difficult bit. As far as our personal continuity goes, we can clearly affirm that we will be physical, embodied people. If you are a male now you will be a male then; if you are a female now you will be a female then; and we will be fully personal. We will be more like we are now than not. If we think back to the last chapter, we can see how our physical resurrection mirrors the renewal of all creation. It is not that all that we know now will be destroyed and a brand new thing will come into existence; if by *brand new* we mean completely different. It is more organic than that. "It will be different as the rich stalk and ear of grain is different from the bare, gnarled little seed from which it grows (1 Cor. 15:35–38)."[26]

A good way to think of this continuity of personal identity is to think back to your conversion to Christ. In some very clear ways at that time you became a "new creature" (2 Cor 5:17). And yet, while it is true we became *new* people when we came to Christ, we still remain the *same* people. At the resurrection the same sort of transformation process will be happen as we—you and I, the people we are, the personalities we are, the identities we carry—will be transformed once more, into the likeness of the risen Christ. We shall be the same . . . but different; different . . . but the same. We will echo the words of Job 19:26–27, "And after my skin has been destroyed, yet in my flesh I will see God; I myself will see him with my own eyes—I, and not another. How my heart yearns within me!" Clearly Job was

25. Alcorn, *Heaven*, 123.
26. Milne, *Know the Truth*, 361.

referring to the fact that the skin he was then wearing would be destroyed, would die and rot, but in the resurrection he will be renewed and made alive, bodily, like Christ.

Despite the fact that all people will be physically resurrected when Christ comes again, and will "be themselves" in every way possible, there is still a level of discontinuity between our bodies now and our bodies then. We can make some general comments about this with certainty. First, life in the new heavens and earth will be free of any sin or the effects of sin: no disease, no suffering, no disabilities, and no death. This is very different from life here, so there is a fundamental discontinuity between our bodies here and our bodies there. Second, in the resurrection we gain some new abilities (Luke 24:31; John 20:19–29). This too is different from our existence now. But we can't press this discontinuity too far. Australian theologian Graham Twelftree speaks of this continuity-discontinuity well:

> [Christ's] body was no longer subject to some of the limitations we presently experience. He could pass through a locked door (Jn 20.19, 26); he could suddenly materialize—at first unrecognized—next to two of his followers (Lk 24.15–16); and he was able to vanish on the Mount of Olives (Acts 1.9). It is this not-too-carefully-described body, released from some of its human limitations, which we can expect to be the model for our bodies in the after-life.[27]

"Will I recognize you, Dad, in Heaven?"

LIAM, AGE 6

In the next few sections we will come back to these themes and develop their implications in more detail.

In addition to a physical and so bodily resurrection, our personal identity will remain. This is the second important truth to make clear in regards to what we will be like. Distinct personal identity continues on in the resurrection. This is an essential truth. Those few individuals who have come back to life and back to earth in the biblical narrative, like Moses and Elijah, are distinct individuals who have retained their identity. We are told that in the new heavens and earth we will sit with distinct people, namely, Abraham and Isaac and others, and share in the great banquet (Matt 8:11). God makes humans—billions of them—with such diversity and skill, and we can be assured that in the resurrection it will not be less diverse but more so than here.

27. Twelftree, *Life After Death*, 116.

It may seem like a truism, but for you to be resurrected it must be a resurrection of *you*. The exact same person who departs this world is the one who goes to be with Christ (Phil 1:23). God created *you*, God redeemed *you*, God has saved *you*, and God will resurrect *you*. It is *you* he wants and it is *you* he will have. Isaiah declared, "'As the new heavens and the new earth that I make will endure before me,' declares the Lord, 'so will your name and descendants endure'" (Isa 66:22). We will retain our identity, our "name," and our relationships, as far as that is possible. Our names reflect our individuality, our personal identity, and our unique selves. On the new earth we will be welcomed by name and will welcome others by name as well. We already see this in part now as we come to Christ and become ever like him; we don't, in that process called sanctification, become less ourselves but in fact more. The truth of Christianity is that the more like Jesus we become in character the more distinct we become in personality.

Let's Talk

In the previous section we saw clearly that God tells us that in the new heavens and earth we will be bodily resurrected to new life, after the pattern of Jesus Christ himself, and our personal identity will carry on for all eternity. In this section we tease out the detail of what these new bodies might mean for us. In the next section we examine some of the trickier questions raised by this material as we play with these concepts.

The first such issue is that of the soul and the body. A lot of ink has been spilled in trying to define what the soul is and what it does. Many believe that we are essentially souls and that our bodies are just incidental features of our earth-bound existence. Such people (and many of them Christians who should know better[28]) are following the teachings of Plato and other philosophers more than those of Christ (and it needs to stop). Genesis 2:7 tells us that God created "man" (in Hebrew, *ādām* is a word that can mean humanity or a male) from the dust of the ground and breathed into his nostrils the breath of life, and at that moment "man" became a "living being." The Hebrew for "living being" is

> "Will we still have birthday parties in Heaven?"
>
> SALLY, AGE 6

28. One study showed that of Americans who believe in a resurrection of the dead, two thirds believe they will not have bodies after the resurrection. *Time* 149, no. 12 (March 24, 1997) 75. I suspect this figure would be matched by evangelicals in other parts of the world, certainly in Oceania, where I work, live, and fellowship.

nephesh hayyah, often translated as "soul" (*psyche* in Greek). *Nephesh* is almost always connected with a form and so it has no existence apart from a body. The best translation that makes sense of what this means then is "person," comprised of physical and spiritual aspects.

Adam became a living being when his physical body and his spirit (breath of God) were united. *Soul* is just one term Holy Scripture uses to speak of a person, the whole person; it is not describing a part of our humanity but the whole of it. It is appropriate to say we are ensouled bodies and embodied souls, living beings who exist in direct dependence upon the life-giving Spirit of God. Your body does not house the *real* you; your body is as much you as anything else. So while Scripture speaks of humans as having bodies, and souls, and spirits, these are just different ways to speak of the complete person, our whole selves. The language was never meant to indicate one could, under the right laboratory conditions (or more likely, in the right theoretical philosophy class), identify, distinguish, and describe one from the other in anything more than a general way.

How can we be so certain of all of this, especially when so many Christians believe we will simply be disembodied spirits (as if that were possible)? The answer is Jesus Christ. Based on the bodily resurrection of our Lord Jesus Christ we have categorical confirmation of what we will be like. We need to take the reality of the resurrected Jesus Christ more seriously in our talk about Heaven. We are told that "now we are children of God, and what we will be has not yet been made known. But we know that when Christ appears, we shall be like him, for we shall see him as he is" (1 John 3:2). So what do we know of Jesus' resurrection that will one day be true of us? We know Jesus was no ghost, if by ghost we mean an apparition, a disembodied spirit, or something like that, for Jesus said to his disciples after his resurrection, "Look at my hands and my feet. It is I myself! Touch me and see; a ghost does not have flesh and bones, as you see I have" (Luke 24:39). For forty days the risen Christ walked the earth, talked with people, and confirmed to them that he was indeed the *same* Jesus Christ who was crucified that was now alive and well. Jesus walked and talked with people (Luke 24:13–35); he was raised to life as a male, the same man he was before the resurrection (John 20:15); he took the disciples for walks along the beach (John 21:4); he cooked them a breakfast of barbeque fish and ate it with them (John 21:12); he wore clothes and he breathed (John 20:22); and he looked, acted, talked, and related to people as an individual. Why then do so many Christians think it is better to be a spirit than a human? As C. S. Lewis argued:

There is no use trying to be more spiritual than God. God never meant man to be a purely spiritual creature. That is why He uses material things like bread and wine to put the new life into us. We may think this rather crude and unspiritual. God does not: He invented eating. He likes matter. He invented it. I know some muddle-headed Christians have talked as if Christianity taught that sex, or the body, or pleasure, were bad in themselves. But they were wrong. Christianity is almost the only one of the great religions which thoroughly approves of the body—which believes that matter is good, that God Himself once took on a human body, and that some kind of body is going to be given to us even in Heaven and is going to be an essential part of our happiness, our beauty, and our energy.[29]

If we press deeper we might want to ask about the nature of our physical resurrected bodies. Are they the exact same bodies we died in (down to the same DNA and molecular structure)? Or are they different bodies, but still, technically speaking, us? Romans 8:11 is a direct affirmation of our bodily and personal continuity: "But if the Spirit of Him who raised Jesus from the dead dwells in you, He who raised Christ Jesus from the dead will also give life to your mortal bodies through His Spirit who dwells in you." In Philippians 3:21 we are told that Jesus "will change our lowly body to be like his glorious body." And in 1 Corinthians 15:37–38 Paul uses the analogy of a seed sown in the ground to indicate the continuity between our mortal bodies and our immortal bodies. In the previous section we examined this in some detail. On the basis of these verses one theologian, Wayne Grudem, affirms, "Whatever remains in the grave from our own physical bodies will be taken by God and transformed and used to make a new resurrection body."[30] Donald Bloesch, another theologian, disagrees. He writes:

> In the resurrection we will not have the very same body that we have now . . . There is no material identity, for the two disciples on the road to Emmaus did not recognize Jesus. I would argue for a formal identity. What we have is a body that corresponds to the physical body, indeed is rooted in it. There is a material continuity but not a reduplication. We should note that though he rose bodily from the dead it is also true that "he appeared in another form" (Mk 16.12). This will surely hold true for all who are in Christ as well.[31]

29. Lewis, "Learning in War-Time," 20–21.
30. Grudem, *Systematic Theology*, 833.
31. Bloesch, *Last Things*, 128–29.

I think Bloesch is correct. If not then we are forced, as many are, to conclude that God will gather up all our molecules and atoms from the last second of our mortal life and reconstitute them into our resurrected bodies (this is in part why many Christians have been opposed to cremation). But this appears to be unnecessary and not stated in Scripture. The difficulties with that view have to do with those who have been dead for many hundreds or many thousands of years. Their bodies have completely degraded, have been distilled into the ground—ground in which crops have subsequently been harvested and then eaten by animals and humans alike. By implication, many of the long dead have been *eaten* by subsequent generations of people (not a pleasant thought, but true nonetheless). If an exact molecular vacuum is required to suck up such molecules and reanimate a person in the resurrection, then many of us will share the same molecules and won't be able to be reconstituted. This is clearly a ludicrous problem. In addition, we note that at the coming of Christ those who are alive will be "changed," not replaced (1 Cor 15:51–53). Also, we know that Christ's resurrected body, though it was the "same" as the body he had before he died, was also somehow different (John 20:20, 27). Again, in Bloesch's words, "We can say that at death the *soma* (body) of the believer is changed from *sarx* (flesh), which by its very essence decays, into *doxa* (glory)—the divine element."[32]

Given it is the same body but different (and hopefully that now makes more sense to you), we might ask about disabilities—physical and mental; will they remain in the resurrection? Theologians are divided on this issue, but where they do agree is that even if some disability remains it will be healed even if not eliminated. Some would argue that Down syndrome, for example, will still exist in the resurrection, but without its limiting effects or frustrations. Others, like myself, would argue that it is more consistent with Scripture to look forward to the total eradication of all disabilities in the resurrection (and every one of us is disabled in one way or another as a result of the fall). That does not have to mean that a person, say, with Down syndrome will be completely different. They won't be. They will be the same person, but changed and renewed. I affirm Joni Erickson Tada's belief that:

> Somewhere in my broken, paralyzed body is the seed of what I shall become. The paralysis makes what I am to become all the more grand when you contrast the atrophied, useless legs against splendorous resurrected legs. I'm convinced that if there are

32. Ibid., 129.

mirrors in heaven (and why not?), the image I'll see will be unmistakably 'Joni', although a much better, brighter Joni.[33]

A related issue having to do with the nature of the resurrected body is that of age, so let us tackle this here. Many people rightly ask what age we will be in the resurrection, and we have been given many answers. The most influential of the medieval theologians, Thomas Aquinas, thought that we would all be resurrected to the same age, around thirty years old, for that was the age Christ was when he was crucified, and it is into his likeness we are conformed. Christian novelist Marilynn Robinson puts this idea onto the lips of one of her characters, Reverend Ames, and has him write in his journal for his young son to read later in life, "I wish I had more pictures of myself as a younger man, I suppose because I believe that as you read this I will not be old, and when I see you, at the end of your good long life, neither of us will be old. We will be like brothers. This is how I imagine it."[34]

Many thinkers have followed his suggestion. And it is a good one, I agree, but I can't accept it. We can't be dogmatic here, of course, but this seems at odds with other things we know to be true of the resurrection. Personally, I find it more convincing to think we shall be resurrected at the same age at which we died, and we will then continue to grow, mature, and even age, as long as we understand that aging in eternity will not be the same as aging now. It appears that Isaiah 11:6–9 supports my case. Even if one thinks this text speaks mostly about a millennial period in world history before the renewal of the earth, they have to concede that in context it also speaks of the new heavens and earth. Isaiah speaks of children and infants being in the new creation (it also does this in Isaiah 65).[35] Given the variety and fecundity of the new creation, it seems to me to be more likely that we will be resurrected to the age we were when we died (or the age we are when Christ returns, if that happens first), and then we will continue to grow. This means that

"Will our bodies get old in Heaven?"

SOPHIE, AGE 5

---

33. Tada, *Heaven*, 39. For a technical defense of the position that disabilities do not remain in the new heavens and new earth see Habets, "Disability and Divinization."

34. Robinson, *Gilead*, 195–96. Later Reverend Ames confirms this belief with the following words: "I believe the soul in Paradise must enjoy something nearer to a perpetual vigorous adulthood than to any other state we know. At least that is my hope. Not that paradise could disappoint, but I believe Boughton is right to enjoy the imagination of heaven as the best pleasure of this world" (Robinson, *Gilead*, 196).

35. For a technical defense of the theology that infants who die will be in the new heavens and earth see Habets, "'Suffer the Little Children to Come to Me."

infants and young children will grow up in the New Jerusalem, and the elderly will continue to grow old. But here I want to remind you of a thought from an earlier chapter: that we will live in God's perfect time and not in fallen time. In fallen time aging means getting older, and after an initial flourish (into our twenties) a gradual diminishing, a deterioration, and finally death. In God's world and in God's time, no such fallen time exists. So what does it mean to celebrate one's one-millionth birthday? Not much, I suspect (besides, that many candles would be a fire hazard).

But aging is only a small part of growth, and it isn't the most important part. Aging has more to do with maturity, development, accomplishment, capacity, and with wisdom. C. S. Lewis is again helpful here as he paints a picture of what it might mean to age in Heaven when in *The Great Divorce* we read, "No one in that company struck me as being of any particular age. One gets glimpses, even in our country, of that which is ageless—heavy thought in the face of an infant, and frolic childhood in that of a very old man. Here it was all like that."[36] What might it mean to live in a place where aging has been redeemed and renewed? It will be a life of progress, I firmly believe, progress and development from one glory to another.

Further evidence for the continuity of personal identity in the resurrection comes from observing the relationships Jesus had with people before his resurrection, and how these relationships developed afterwards as well. Here we might think of his friends Mary Magdalene (John 20:10–18), Thomas (John 20:24–49), and Peter (John 21:15–22). When we come to reflect on this theologically and then play with these ideas later in the chapter, this will become a precious and important point for us. And what is true of Christ will be true of us!

Some might say at this point, "What about the fact that Jesus could walk through locked doors (John 20:19) and do other things human bodies can't do now?" And that would be a good question, and one that points towards the discontinuity of our resurrected bodies with the ones we have now. We will examine this aspect of our life later in the chapter, but for now I simply want to assert that, while there will be differences, the bodies we are to receive will be glorious and more powerful than the ones we have now, but our embodiment and personal identity will remain.

36. Lewis, *Great Divorce*, 24.

Related to the issue of our own personal identity is another question that arises—that of personal recognition. Will we recognize other people there? Yes, of course we will, because we know them here. And in God's city we will know and be known to a far greater extent than we ever could in this life. Given the continuity of personal identity and the ability to recognize others on the new earth, I personally look forward to meeting my wife and children, parents, wider family, and friends in Heaven, not to mention all the Christians from history

"How will we recognize each other in Heaven?"

SYDNEY, AGED 9

and in Scripture that I want to talk with. This will be one of the best parts of life in God's city: spending time with fellow believers, in God's company.

But more interesting than this, how will we recognize those we have never met, perhaps great grandparents who died before we were born and others? Well, we get a glimpse of what it might be like from the animal kingdom. My home country of New Zealand has four million people and thirty million sheep. While sheep do have some visible differences, they basically all look the same to us. It turns out that sheep have quite an advanced ability at facial recognition. Many animals look nearly identical to each other and yet parents can find their children easily enough using senses other than sight. Sometimes they identify each other by smell, but often we are simply stumped by how they do it. For other animals, is it a distinct personal electro-magnetic signature? Bats use sonar, don't they? We simply don't know how we will do it. I would like to think that in the new heavens and earth we will know people instinctively, not simply by sight but relationally, by the Holy Spirit. As the disciples instantly recognized Moses and Elijah on the Mount of Transfiguration (remember, this predated photos and video technology) (Luke 9:28–36), so I think we will "recognize" saints in Heaven. Anthony Thiselton hints at the same thing when he writes, "after the resurrection of the 'body' (sōma), this will not be by physical sight or sound or by recognition through the senses, but will be by some *hitherto unspecified* counterpart to what served for these purposes in the present life."[37] We will know people for who they really are and not simply by the way they look. For those parents who have lost children or for children who have lost parents at an early age, we will see our family, we will know our family, we will recognize them

"Can I still go to school in Heaven?"

MICAH, AGED 5

37. Thiselton, *Systematic Theology*, 376 (emphasis in original).

for who they really are. And there will be great rejoicing in Heaven and on the earth.

Or perhaps it is far simpler than that; maybe there are name tags we have to wear for an age or two, or perhaps this is one of the angels' jobs, to be heavenly ushers for us (Luke 16:22). This last point is semi-serious, actually; we know that angels look over us on earth (Ps 91:11): they know when we are saved and rejoice in Heaven (Luke 15:10), and they know when we die and bring us to God (Luke 16:22). So it is not unreasonable to think that in the intermediate state (Heaven) and in the new heavens and earth they would prepare loved ones so that there might be an arrival party at the pearly gates. Christian comedian Thor Ramsey reflects on this when he gives the following satirical reflection. "Can you imagine seeing a long-dead loved one? I bet the first time you see them you'll scream and jump for joy, then laugh, then cry, just like girls at a cheerleading competition."[38] I believe I will do just that!

But we can dig still deeper again and ask what this might mean for those of us who are married. We know there is no marriage or giving in marriage in the new heavens and earth (Matt 22:30). Given the fact that in Holy Scripture sexual intercourse is reserved for married couples, we can confidently affirm there is no sex on the new earth. This does not mean we stop being male or female in Heaven. For many Christians, our resurrected bodies more resemble a Barbie or Ken doll than they do the human bodies we will have in the resurrection. With all the plastic genital ambiguity of Mattel's Ken, many Christians think we will be more like androgynous plastic dolls than the physical and gendered beings we currently are (I always did prefer Action Man to Ken). But they are wrong. We will be the men or women God created us to be.

Procreation won't be required in the New Jerusalem, so sex is out. But sexual intercourse in this life means far more than a physical act. God the Father knows this (Gen 2:24), Jesus knows this (Mark 10:8), and Paul knows this (1 Cor 6:15). Sexual intercourse is a very temporal, physical act that has eternal and emotional consequences. The intimacy, vulnerability, and deep relational satisfaction we gain through sexual intercourse is but a pale shadow of the real intimacy, vulnerability, and deep relational satisfaction we shall experience from the triune God and from the community we will enjoy in the resurrection. This is why Thor Ramsey says, with full

38. Ramsey, *Comedian's Guide to Theology*, 227.

comedic intent, "Theology is better than sex."[39] We can turn to C. S. Lewis
again at this point for help. Lewis uses the analogy of a young boy who
loves eating chocolates. When he is told that "The sexual act is the highest
bodily pleasure," the boy immediately asks, "Do you eat chocolates at the
same time?" When he is told no, he is dumbfounded and crestfallen. "In
vain would you tell him that the reason why lovers in their carnal raptures
don't bother about chocolates is that they have something better to think of.
The boy knows chocolate: he does not know the positive thing that excludes
it. We are in the same position."[40] In the resurrection we will have desires
fulfilled that we don't even know we have yet, and that will put sex in its
place as a reality only for the present world, not the one to come.

Will we be married in the resurrection? That is a slightly different
question than the one above. Put differently, Will I see my wife, Odele, know
who she is, and know what she means to me (she is my beloved) on the new
earth? I think it impossible to believe that I will know Odele and not know
she was my wife on the old earth. I find it impossible to believe that I will
see my children and not know they are my children as opposed to anybody
else's, or worse still, no one's. So yes, I think something of our relationships
here will remain for eternity, but they will carry on in very different ways.
The exclusive relationship I have with my wife now is but a foretaste of the
communal and non-sexual nature of life in eternity. Scripture says as much
when it likens marriage to Christ and the church (Eph 5:31–32). The oneness we feel in a loving marriage relationship will one day be eclipsed as all
those resurrected to live with God in Christ experience oneness with God.

Keeping consistent with this impetus of biblical revelation, I think we
also need to be clear on the idea of perpetual human progress, growth, and
maturity in all things, not simply aging. Wayne Grudem once postulated:

> . . . Since God is infinite and we can never exhaust his greatness
> (Ps. 145:3), and since we are finite creatures who will never equal
> God's knowledge or be omniscient, we may expect that for all eter-
> nity we will be able to go on learning more about God and about
> his relationship to his creation. In this way we will continue the
> process of learning that was begun in this life, in which a life "fully

39. Ibid., 16. He goes on to say, "This statement may come as good news to nuns
across America, but how does it help you and me . . ."

40. Lewis, *Miracles*, 260–61.

pleasing to him" is one that includes continually "increasing in the knowledge of God" (Col. 1:10).[41]

"Will we have wings in Heaven?"

LIAM, AGE 4

The idea of perpetual human progress is one of the most exciting parts of this story. To be human is, in part, to grow mentally, emotionally, physically, and psychologically (to name just a few features). Why would life in the resurrection be any different? Certainly not because we are perfect.

Many people think being perfect means we become everything we were ever intended to be, we cannot get any better, and we cannot change at all. In short, something perfect has to remain just as it is, without change in any way. That, I suggest, would be incorrect when it comes to creation. Perfect is a relative term when used of creatures or creation. When we use the word *perfect* for anything in creation we have to ask: Perfect for what? I often use the illustration of an automobile and ask: What is the perfect automobile? I once had a student who drove a sports car. The class could see it from the lecture room and it was a beauty. The student was single, and the car had two seats. It was perfect. A few years later the same student, now married, came to college in a four-door saloon (it was *not* a beauty). We asked why. He told us that with a child on the way they needed a new vehicle. They now had the perfect vehicle for them. So what is the perfect automobile? It depends on what you want it for. As far as I am concerned, a Harley-Davidson CVO Street Glide Special is about as fine a vehicle as you could ever wish to have (and I do hold out a very definite hope I shall ride one on the new earth). But with a wife and two young children it simply is not the perfect vehicle for me now.

So in answer to the question "Will we be perfect in Heaven?" we have to say yes. But the nature of creaturely perfection means we will continue to change and develop, and continue to be perfected in a multitude of ways. We will exhibit perfect concentration, perfect determination, perfect skills of deduction, perfect emotions, perfect patience, and perfect thoughts, but that does not imply a static existence—quite the opposite. It speaks to a life fully alive to God and others.[42]

41. Grudem, *Systematic Theology*, 1162.

42. Anthony Thiselton has a helpful reflection on this: "If God himself characterizes heaven, there we should expect to participate in his dynamic, purposive, ongoing life. This is precisely confirmed by the concept of 'the resurrection of the body' (sōma pneumatikon), which the Holy Spirit enlivens and sustains. It is frequently said that the authentic experience of the Holy Spirit is of One who is ever-fresh, ever-new, and onward

Will we know everything and feel everything? No. That is reserved for God. If we knew everything and felt everything (to name but two aspects of living) we would be equal to God in every way and that is not only idolatrous, it is also silly. Imagine the following scenario: you find yourself in the resurrection and you know all that can ever be known and you have the ability to solve every puzzle (so there actually are no puzzles), to achieve every goal (so there are no goals), and to do whatever you want. Being almost equal to the being of God in every possible way, what is the first thing we would do? We would turn our backs on God and look for something new, something different, something *other*. And that right there is the definition of the original sin: turning from God to something other. No, God has made us perfectly in order to become ever more perfected. And the new earth is the place God has designed for this to happen. We have occasion to look into this in more detail in the next chapter.

While life on the new earth will be restful, as the next chapter will detail, whether we are working or playing, the question of sleep arises. In this life we sleep because we have to. It is essential to good health. But on the new earth we won't *need* to sleep. Our bodies will not need to recover or rejuvenate in the same way. Our conscious minds won't need to switch off in order to keep sane. Sydney, my daughter, loves to sleep. She asked me the other day if I think she will be able to sleep in Heaven. I replied, "Yes honey, I believe you will. But not because you have to, simply because you might want to." I also went on to say that if life on the new earth is as active and exciting as I think it will be (read the next chapter), then I think we will want to sleep at times, to relax and nestle into a soft bed and a soft pillow. That is one of the great joys of life here for those fortunate enough to have a roof over their head and a bed to sleep in. I can't see why it wouldn't be one of the joys of our new life too.

The consistent teaching of Holy Scripture is that we will always have bodies, even though they will be glorious, Spirit-filled bodies fashioned after that of Christ's resurrected one, and that our personality and character, while redeemed, will continue on the new earth. In the final section we play with these ideas and address some important questions raised about such

---

going. Thus there would be nothing static or 'fixed' about life animated and sustained by the Holy Spirit, after death. 'After' the resurrection of the dead, and 'after' the Last Judgment, life (Gk. zōē) will be like a flowing river, rather than a static pool (Rev. 22:1–2). Raised believers will experience the purposive, progressive, new creation." Thiselton, *Systematic Theology*, 374 (emphasis in original).

matters and bring our Christian imaginations to bear on what we might be like there.

Let's Play

There are at least five things we can say about what we will be like in the new heavens and earth. First, it will be an embodied life. We shall be raised to new life with new resurrection bodies that will be immortal and glorious like that of Jesus Christ (1 Cor 15:35–37). Life will thus be lived as a male or a female, with arms and legs, lips and ankles, and although we may have enhanced powers suitable to life in eternity, we will be very much like we are now.

Second, all the images of the new heavens and earth are social images (it is noticeable that many of the images of Hell are ones of isolation). The new earth is a perfect city (Heb 13:14), the kingdom of God (Heb 12:28), a holy temple (Ezekiel 40–48), a wedding feast (Rev 19:7), and so forth. Humans were created for community and the new earth is the zenith or fulfillment of all right relationships.

Third, life on the new earth will involve to some degree a level of responsibility, and by that I mean we will be given jobs to do; there will be tasks to perform, work to enjoy, labor to employ, and things to achieve. We are told that we will serve God there (Rev 22:3), even if the exact details of that service are not spelled out. When speaking in parables Jesus alluded to the fact that on the new earth we will be given tasks to perform (Luke 19:11–26), and Paul consistently taught that resurrected believers will have work to do (1 Cor 6:2). We deal with this in the next chapter.

Fourth, life on the new earth will be one lived without sin, without the sickening effects of the fall, and in the absence of anything that would tempt us away from glorifying the triune God. Life then will be one of eternal progress and perfecting, as we go from glory to glory. In the new heavens and earth, as we have previously stated, we will find a perfection and perfecting of our relationship with the triune God, with each other, and with all of creation (Ps 8:4–6).

Fifth, having already considered in the previous chapter the idea of eternity being both a quality and a duration, we can now affirm that we shall be with God in glory for all time, with no possibility of falling into sin again and no possibility of anything storming the kingdom of God and bringing it to an end.

Given all that we now know of our coming resurrection existence, we are well placed to answer a few other questions about what we will be like there. Colton Burpo, the boy I mentioned in the introduction who claimed to have been to Heaven and came back to tell the story, thought that in the resurrection we will get wings and have halos over our heads. Nowhere in Scripture is that view supported. The halos come from art history more than anywhere else (and perhaps from the idea that our appearance will be glorious, bright shining as the sun) and the idea that we would have wings is simply a confusion of humans for angels. So we can dispel some of these fanciful ideas immediately. But other questions are asked and we are now well placed to offer some possible answers.

Musician Eric Clapton lost his four-year-old son, Conor, who died after falling from the fifty-third-floor window of a New York City apartment his mother was living in. In order to aid his healing Clapton cowrote the song "Tears in Heaven." In the opening stanza Clapton sings, "Would you know my name / If I saw you in heaven? Would it be the same / If I saw you in heaven? I must be strong / And carry on / 'Cause I know I don't belong / Here in heaven."[43] Clapton wrote about this song in his 2007 autobiography:

> "Will we have to wait in line to see God?"
>
> CINDY, AGED 8

The most powerful of the new songs was "Tears in Heaven." Musically, I had always been haunted by Jimmy Cliff's song "Many Rivers to Cross" and wanted to borrow from that chord progression, but essentially I wrote this one to ask the question I had been asking myself ever since my grandfather had died. Will we really meet again? It's difficult to talk about these songs in depth, that's why they're songs. Their birth and development is what kept me alive through the darkest period of my life. When I try to take myself back to that time, to recall the terrible numbness that I lived in, I recoil in fear. I never want to go through anything like that again. Originally, these songs were never meant for publication or public consumption; they were just what I did to stop from going mad. I played them to myself, over and over, constantly changing or refining them, until they were part of my being.[44]

43. Eric Clapton (cowritten with Will Jennings), "Tears in Heaven," from the soundtrack to *Rush* (Warner Brothers, 1992).

44. Sourced online (because someone never gave back my copy of Clapton's autobiography. If you are that person, give it back!), http://www.songfacts.com/detail.php?id=1274.

Like Clapton, countless numbers of people want to know if they will see their loved ones again. Children are especially passionate about this and often ask if they will see Mum and Dad again after they have died. We now know we can give an assured yes to their questions. If someone loves the Lord Jesus Christ they will be resurrected to eternal life in the new heavens and earth and there will be great reunions when we get there.

Earlier I introduced the idea of perpetual progress in eternity and what that might mean for aging. It would be fun to play around with the idea of aging. Imagine a conversation with our children about what we might look like when we meet on the new earth. What could it mean to see grandparents not as old withered things (I know not all grandparents are old and withered, and my mother and mother-in-law *certainly* aren't, but to a child they often appear so) but as older than us but carrying a quality of youthfulness that makes them appear younger than they are? We might go on to ask them how they might recognize us if we look slightly different than we do now. If they can't imagine that then play a game with them: turn the lights off and tell them they have to guess who is who. Clearly, they will recognize our voice, or laugh, or smell, or touch. This could be a really good teachable moment about how our personal identity is bound up with much more than outward appearance. If you like movies then you might even consider watching *The Shaggy Dog*. The original 1959 movie may be a bit dull for them but the 2006 remake should be okay. Look especially at how the children were able to recognize their father despite the fact that he had turned into a sheepdog.[45] Now make the point that in the resurrection we will be more like ourselves now than not; that is, we won't look like shaggy dogs! That should be a reassuring thought.

You might like to contemplate what it might mean for our five senses to be working at 100 percent, unfiltered by the effects of the fall. We could ask our children to imagine what it would be like to see, smell, touch, taste, and hear with crystal clarity. Better still, have a deaf relative or friend present and see how they respond to this good news. We already know how people responded to Christ's healing of deafness, blindness, and paralysis; they jumped for joy, hugged and kissed their relatives and friends, and lived enhanced lives. The best of them also thanked Christ for what he had done. In the resurrection the transformation and renewal of all people will be like that, but more intense and more profound.

45. *The Shaggy Dog* (Disney, 2006).

Personally, I am terribly color-defective (popularly known as being "color-blind"). Greens, browns, and reds look the same to me; and blues, purples, and some greens look similar too; and the rest of the color spectrum appears to me washed out and dull. They say Van Gogh, the Dutch post-impressionist artist, had cataracts and glaucoma and this in part explains why later in life his paintings were opaque and dominated by halos and yellows. I think that is how people like myself with severe color-defectiveness see the world. One day a colleague, also severely color-defective, came to work with a new pair of glasses. But these were no ordinary glasses. He had visited an optometrist and was fitted with color-correcting lenses.[46] While not calibrated for me, he let me try them out for ten minutes. I put them on and walked outside and . . . *bang*! I could see a vibrancy in the flowers that I had never experienced before. An ambulance roared down the road and I could see its flashing lights for what seemed like miles and miles. On the ground some distance from me was one of the brightest objects I had ever seen in my life. I didn't recognize it until I walked up to it and realized it was a fluorescent orange traffic safety cone. Who knew they were so bright?! I was gobsmacked. For the first time in my life I experienced something of the way most other people see the world. My thoughts went straight to the resurrection. Then I shall see fully.

What "disabilities" do you have? (I use the word *disability* here in a very general sense to indicate anything that is underdeveloped here but will be fully developed there.) Imagine out loud with your children how life with God on the new earth will be experienced differently. This would be a good exercise to tease out and play with the idea of the discontinuity we will experience in the resurrection. Will we walk through closed doors like Christ did? Could we walk on water there? What else might we be able to do?

You might also like to ask about those physical and personal traits we each have—those things that make us different from others—that we could imagine continuing into the resurrection. Will introverts still be introverts? I believe so, because being an introvert is not a part of fallen creation; it is who you are (the same goes for us loud extroverts, believe it or not). Will my freckles remain? Perhaps. Perhaps not. See if you can come up with an intelligent and faithful discussion about why they may or may not remain. Remember, our self-image will be healed and those glossy fashion

46. The *New York Times* ran an article about these lenses. See http://www.nytimes .com/2000/02/08/health/a-new-technology-that-colors-the-world-sort-of.html.

magazines that modern Western culture so prizes now are most definitely not going to be published there (it is not that they are entirely evil, but that they promote low self-esteem, narcissism, and vanity). Gone will be the vain attempts to measure ourselves according to the perceptions of other people. Only Christ's opinion counts.

Will the scar on my back be there, the one I received from falling on a corrugated iron fence I was climbing over? I'm not sure, but I have a theory. We know that between his resurrection and ascension the Lord Jesus carried the marks of his crucifixion on his body (John 20:27). What we don't know is whether he carried these with him into glory (theologians are divided over this question). We can't be dogmatic about this but I suspect he did not, or if he did they have since healed over and disappeared with the progress of eternal time. As to my scar, it may be there initially, but I doubt it will endure. I believe the same about most other forms of physical and mental disabilities as well.

What will endure is our character, or distinct personality. C. S. Lewis imagined what this might look like when he penned his wonderful little book *The Great Divorce*, a juicy allegory in which he has a busload of people from Hell go on a day trip to Heaven. The people from "grey town" (Hell) enter Heaven (the new earth, I believe), and there they find they are less physical, less "real," less human, than the inhabitants of Heaven. To Lewis the people of grey town look transparent; "they were in fact ghosts: man-shaped stains on the brightness of that air."[47] The terrain and people of Heaven, by contrast, are solid, real, and very physical. The narrator tries to pluck a daisy growing at his feet only to find he is not strong enough to do so. He tries to pick up a leaf but it is too heavy for him to lift. The green grass that looks beautiful is too painful to walk on. Although this world (the new earth) is the most glorious they have ever seen, every feature of the landscape (the flowers, grass, and water) is unyieldingly solid compared to themselves. However, for the inhabitants of the new earth—the "bright people," those redeemed and savingly united to Christ and living in resurrected bodies—the new earth is sweet and pleasant and fits them perfectly.

> . . . I saw people coming to meet us. Because they were bright I
> saw them while they were still very distant, and at first I did not
> know that they were people at all. Mile after mile they drew nearer.
> The earth shook under their tread as their strong feet sank into
> the wet turf. A tiny haze and a sweet smell went up where they

47. Lewis, *Great Divorce*, 20.

56

had crushed the grass and scattered the dew. Some were naked, some were robed. But the naked ones did not seem less adorned, and the robes did not disguise in those who wore them the massive grandeur of muscle and radiant smoothness of flesh. Some were bearded but no one in that company struck me as being of any particular age. One gets glimpses, even in our country, of that which is ageless—heavy thought in the face of an infant, and frolic childhood in that of a very old man. Here it was all like that.[48]

Lewis is playing, of course, but what play it is. I hope you can already discern in his playful description some of the things we have explored in this chapter: the splendor of the resurrection, the physical nature of our bodily existence, the fact of age and gender differences, and of personal identity and distinction, but also of Christlikeness, and a certain level of bodily discontinuity. In the next chapter we look at what we will do in the new heavens and earth.

Summary

In this chapter I have tried to communicate the following:

- All people will be resurrected with physical bodies.
- There is no such thing as a disembodied soul.
- Individual, personal identity will endure for all eternity.
- Jesus Christ is the pattern of our resurrection.
- Our resurrected bodies will exhibit both continuity and discontinuity with our bodies now.
- There will be continued growth and development in eternity.
- We will recognize each other on the new earth.
- There will be no disability, sickness, disease, sadness, or sin there.
- The relationships we form now will somehow survive into eternity.

48. Ibid., 23–24.

Chapter 4

An Endless Adventure

(What Will We Do in the New Jerusalem?)

There is a place called "heaven" where the good here unfinished
is completed; and where the stories unwritten, and the hopes
unfulfilled, are continued. We may laugh together yet . . .[1]

J. R. R. TOLKIEN, LETTER TO HIS SON MICHAEL

"You do not yet look so happy as I mean you to be."

Lucy said, "We're so afraid of being sent away, Aslan. And
you have sent us back into our own world so often."

"No fear of that," said Aslan. "Have you not guessed?"

Their hearts leaped and a wild hope rose within them.

"There was a real railway accident," said Aslan softly. "Your
father and mother and all of you are—as you used to call it in
the Shadowlands—dead. The term is over: the holidays have
begun. The dream is ended: this is the morning."

And as he spoke he no longer looked to them like a lion; but
things that began to happen after that were so great and beautiful that I cannot write them. And for us this is the end of all the
stories, and we can most truly say that they all lived happily ever
after. But for them it was only the beginning of the real story.
All their life in this world and all their adventures in Narnia

---

1. Tolkien, "Letter to Michael Tolkien, 9 June 1941," 55.

had only been the cover and the title page: now at last they were beginning Chapter One of the Great Story which no one on earth has read: which goes on forever: in which every chapter is better than the one before.[2]

Vapid (lifeless and uninspiring) is one way to describe how many view the new heavens and earth. We are learning that the reality is very different. The new heavens and earth will be a renewed creation, more vast, expansive, colorful, and exciting that any world we know of here; and in this world we will be physically and bodily resurrected and made fit for living there. In this chapter we look at what on earth we will be doing for all eternity in the new heavens and earth. But hold on to your seats, for this is where it really gets exciting. You are going to love discussing this with your children (and other passionate believers).

Let's Listen

Knowing that we will have physical resurrected bodies and that our personal identity will be continued in the new heavens and earth, we now have to ask what it is we will do there, for all eternity. We have already anticipated some of the responses to this question, but there is more—a lot more.

Two images or teachings in Scripture about our eternal state dominate when we come to consider what we will be doing in the new heavens and earth. Namely, we shall be active and we shall be resting. On the surface it seems as if these are two contradictory images, but upon closer inspection we find they aren't. One can work and then rest, of course, and that makes perfect sense. But Scripture is more complex than that and the way it speaks of rest and of work need to be teased out a little so we don't slip into any false notions.

First, let us examine the biblical idea of *rest*. Scripture regularly uses the idea of rest as an image of eternal life. But what does it mean? In John 14:2 we are told there are many "resting places"; Revelation 14:13 promises "rest from our labors"; and Hebrews 4:9 speaks of a "Sabbath rest" remaining for the people of God. In the New Testament rest is not the cessation

2. Lewis, *Last Battle*, 171–72 (HarperCollins).

of all activity, nor complete motionlessness. It is relative, by contrast to the sort of activity that has preceded it. That activity is the spiritual warfare of the believer here on earth: the battle against the world, the flesh, and the devil. Such activity is compared to a fight (1 Tim 6:12), to a race (1 Cor 9:24), to running (Heb 12:1), and to wrestling (Eph 6:12). And so rest is not the cessation of all activity but the experience of reaching a goal of crucial importance. As such, Heaven is the completion of the Christian pilgrimage, the end of the *struggle* against all forms of sin and evil. There will be work to do, but it will not involve fighting against opposing forces. Rest then equals the cessation from all opposition. It is not the rest of something that has wound itself down to stillness; it is rest from endurance against evil. This approximates some of the meaning of the Hebrew word *shalom* (peace or wholeness). Our experience of the new earth will be one of absolute shalom.

Now this is not to be taken as implying we will be constantly active in the resurrection. We shall rest in a second sense also: relaxation and rejuvenation. After God created the world in six days he rested on the seventh (Gen 2:2). This resting becomes the paradigm for the observance of Sabbath for the people of God (Lev 25:4–5). To rest and relax is important for us; it gives us perspective, balance, and brings peace. The New Jerusalem will be a place of peace, that home in which we respond to Jesus' invitation to come to him and find rest (Matt 11:28).

We shall rest and we shall work. The creation and calling of humanity is to serve God, to glorify God, to enjoy and be delighted in God. What activities will we be engaged in? It would be a mistake to think of Heaven as being a place for mere self-indulgence or self-gratification. Scripture affirms that in the new heavens and earth believers will be given added responsibilities to those here on earth, in God's service. One of the things we will be doing—the most important thing—is worshipping the triune God of grace and glory. Regular worship of God seems to constitute much of our time in Heaven (Isa 6:3; Rev 19:1–8). Our worship and praise here and now are preparation and practice for future employment of our hearts and voices. We shall pray (which is simply talking with God), sing, and praise God, and in so doing we shall know that this is what we were created to do from the beginning.

We know, however, that worship involves more than singing and praying. Worship is not only a verbal, emotional expression of praise. It includes all that we do for God's glory and fame. Historically in the West, the contemplation or worship of God in the resurrection has been described as the beatific vision (Matt 5:8; 2 Cor 3:12–18). In the East, it has more regularly been described as participating in the Divine nature (John 17:20–21; 2 Pet 1–4). The *beatific vision* has to do with seeing God and, in that vision, contemplating what cannot be known. It is about losing oneself in God's splendor in contemplative meditation. That will clearly be part of what we do on the new earth. However, this can and often is thought to be too static or too passive. I prefer the Eastern vision of participation, of sharing in the very life of the triune God, and in this sharing finding ourselves to be eternally happy. Perhaps we don't have to choose between the two options, though. The *beatific vision* is really meant to express the same reality as participation in God's nature.

> The beatific vision is *the full union of the human person with God.* It is that toward which every person strives. It is that which transcends the person on this earth and draws the person beyond himself or herself to become something other than he or she is at present. It is the goal of every human inquiry, search, and gesture toward the other. "Our hearts are restless," Augustine cried out to God, "until they rest in Thee."[3]

We discuss in what ways we may worship God more fully in the next section.

In addition to worship, there will be all manner of work to do: life-giving, energy-producing, soul-enlarging work. First, Holy Scripture teaches us about rewards that will be given out based on our faithfulness in this life. There is a strong compensatory aspect to the new heavens and earth in the biblical view. It is not a compensation for the loss in this world, like some eternal life insurance or cosmic karma, but rather the compensation of justice. In the new heavens and earth the wrongs that Christ's people have endured will be righted. So Heaven is necessary, and the fact that the righteous may suffer in this life while the wicked prosper is an argument in favor of there being a Heaven to come. All who are in Heaven are there due to one factor—divine grace. No one will be in Heaven on account of their own works (merit), or for their own intrinsic worth (they deserve it). They will be there because, in his grace, the Father decided to apply the

> "Are there toys in Heaven?"
>
> JASON, AGE 3

3. McBrien, *Catholicism*, 1142.

benefits of Christ's life, death, and resurrection to them through the Spirit, appropriated by the believer by grace through faith (Eph 2:8).

If we can understand the basis upon which all of us enter into God's renewed world, then the question of rewards will come into right perspective. Scripture is quite clear that there will be a sort of first among equals in the resurrection. Even though we are all there by grace, nevertheless, some will enjoy greater rewards than others (at least for a time). I think it fair to say that we enter the New Jerusalem on the basis of grace alone, but we are adorned in there on the basis of the fruits of our faith. We see this in Jesus' answer to a mother's question in Matthew 20:23 and in many of the parables (Matt 13:8 for instance). Luke 6:35 clearly speaks of rewards as something earned by the believer while living on earth. This is quite consistent with what has already been said about Heaven being in a sense continuous with earth, not unrelated.

Paul is emphatic about the fact that what we do now, and how we live our lives on earth, will have an effect on how we will live on the new earth. In 2 Corinthians 5:10 we read, "For we must all appear before the judgment seat of Christ, so that each of us may receive what is due us for the things done while in the body, whether good or bad." He elaborates on this in 1 Corinthians 3:10–15:

> By the grace God has given me, I laid a foundation as a wise builder, and someone else is building on it. But each one should build with care. For no one can lay any foundation other than the one already laid, which is Jesus Christ. If anyone builds on this foundation using gold, silver, costly stones, wood, hay or straw, their work will be shown for what it is, because the Day will bring it to light. It will be revealed with fire, and the fire will test the quality of each person's work. If what has been built survives, the builder will receive a reward. If it is burned up, the builder will suffer loss but yet will be saved—even though only as one escaping through the flames.

Note carefully that entrance to eternal life with God is on the basis of grace and faith, not works. Note also that the foundation is Jesus Christ and what he has accomplished for us. Our contribution is merely what is built on that foundation, or what we do with the salvation we have been given. It is this latter work that is judged and rewarded. (Revelation 20:11–15 contains a parallel vision of what those not savingly united to Christ will experience. They will not be permitted into eternal life with God, based on their lack of faith in response to God's grace, and only then are their works judged.

Unbelievers face God before the Great White Throne, believers face our Lord and Savior Jesus Christ before the Bema/Judgment Seat. The point here is that, for believers and unbelievers alike, what we do in this life has a bearing on what we will do in the next.)

One way Holy Scripture describes this aspect of rewards in the new heavens and earth is with the imagery of crowns. There are five heavenly crowns mentioned in the New Testament that will be awarded to believers. They are the imperishable crown (1 Cor 9:24–25), the crown of rejoicing (1 Thess 2:19), the crown of righteousness (2 Tim 4:8), the crown of glory (1 Pet 5:4), and the crown of life (Rev 2:10). In New Testament times a crown was either a badge of royalty, a prize in the public games, or a symbol of high honor. Paul loves sports imagery and so it is possible he had in mind the wreath of leaves placed on the victor's head at athletic contests. As such, Paul uses the idea of crowns figuratively for the rewards God promises those who are faithful. Joni Erickson Tada playfully speaks of these crowns as "God's party favors."[4]

A final image that speaks to rewards is that of treasure. Jesus told us to "store up for yourselves treasures in heaven" (Matt 6:20). He went on to make it clear that such treasure is not sought for narcissistic or selfish reasons, but is the (super)natural response of God's love for us: "Where your treasure is, there your heart will be also" (Matt 6:21). Jesus says that he will bring rewards with him when he returns (Rev 22:12). Rewards will be given for work done here on earth, but the point of our motivations must be made clear. The only valid motive for service is that of glorifying God. The *Westminster Confession* asks:

> "What is there in Heaven? Is there trees?"
>
> LILY GRACE, AGED 4

> "Q1: What is the chief end of humanity?
> Answer: To glorify God by enjoying him forever."[5]

Here is the key to how we can be rewarded in Heaven on the basis of *grace*, not merit. We serve Christ based on the motivation that we shall be rewarded in Heaven. What is the essence of reward in Heaven? It is surely intimacy with God, it is responsibilities in which we shall prove and reveal

4. Cited by Martindale, *Beyond the Shadowlands*, 43.

5. I have, with many others, slightly adapted the original wording of the Confession to bring out its intended meaning more forcefully; from "glorify God and enjoy him forever" to "to glorify God by enjoying him forever."

our intimacy with God, and it is to glorify God more abundantly in the life to come than here in our fallen life on earth. Heavenly rewards must, it would seem to me, include an increased opportunity to glorify God through acts of joyous service. "If crowns are suggested, it is only to imply that we will be given tasks of exhilarating importance and fascination."[6] Hence, reward is a powerful motive for Christian living as it will bring increased joy and pleasure on the new earth. However, that increased joy and pleasure is in glorifying God more in the life to come than it is possible now in this life on earth. Rewards are always by grace and never due to our human merit. As Paul Helm concluded, "What ought to motivate the believer is the reward of being completely renovated in Christ and of fulfilling the divinely-assigned role in heaven. Who could say that such a desire is sinful or immoral?"[7]

The idea of rewards and of differences among the saints in eternity often causes some to speculate about the possible effects of envy. But a moment's reflection will show the impossibility of this. The new heavens and earth are a place of supreme joy and fulfillment for all who are there, based upon the sufficiency and fullness of the work of Christ. Part of that joy will be to rest in the sovereign appointments of God, a willingness that is itself the product of divine grace.

A second key activity for us in the new heavens and earth, in addition to serving God through the issuance of rewards, is our participation in the work of divine judgment. Paul says categorically in 1 Corinthians 6:2–3, "Or do you not know that the Lord's people will judge the world? And if you are to judge the world, are you not competent to judge trivial cases? Do you not know that we will judge angels? How much more the things of this life!" That is one amazing text! To think that you and I will one day help God in judging the world and the angels—you and me! At our best we know we are not fit to judge anything or anyone. Rather, it is *we* who need to be judged. But God says that in the resurrection you and I will now be fit to judge others. We shall be wise enough, discerning enough, and holy enough to make good and sound judgments after God's own. It is clear that we won't be doing this sort of work for all eternity. Rather, judgment is limited to that complex period at the end of world history as we know it (Rev 20:4; Matt 19:28; Luke 22:30). This work of judgment has already begun, in fact, when we consider that throughout history God has established people to act as

6. Martindale, *Beyond the Shadowlands*, 40.

7. Helm, *Last Things*, 107.

wise judges over others. Here we might think of Moses as the leader of the Hebrews in the exile, or the judges in ancient Israel, or human governments over civil affairs, or elders in the church. What thrills me so much about this vision is not the actual act of judging others, or ruling more generally, but the fact that we will be fit and worthy judges. That is the miracle. What God first entrusted to Adam and Eve in the garden of Eden will now be fulfilled by you and me in the resurrection. Under Christ's cosmic rule we too shall be given responsibility and privilege. In the resurrection as with now, service is a reward, not a chore or a punishment.

From rest, reward, and ruling we turn to some non-r words that speak to what we will do for eternity. Scripture tells us that we will be involved in other activity as well, including but not limited to eating, drinking, resting, working, exploring, playing, learning, growing, maturing, hosting, and visiting. The first thing we will hear when we enter the new heavens and new earth is the popping of a cork on a wine bottle, followed by a grand party. In the new heavens and earth, we shall, as physical beings, be eating and drinking, just as we are told we would in Scripture (Rev 9:9). Jesus told us he will once again drink wine with his followers in the heavenly kingdom (Luke 22:18). The river of life will flow through the middle of the city (Rev 22.1) and the tree of life will bear twelve kinds of fruit each month (Rev 22:2). We will eat "hidden manna"—whatever that might be, but we can be sure it will be delicious (Rev 2:17)—and we will eat fruit off the tree of eternal life—which many think may be tomatoes and not apples, but I don't think it will be either (Rev 2:7).

As indicated in the previous chapter, there is no good reason to consider these images of eating and drinking as simply symbols of non-physical realities. It is more consistent to believe that in the new heavens and earth we shall be frequenting banquets, parties, and many celebrations. Wayne Grudem asks rhetorically, "Are symbolic banquets and symbolic wine and symbolic rivers and trees somehow superior to real banquets and real wine and real rivers and trees in God's eternal plan?"[8] No, they aren't. And the delights of the new earth will be more, not less, than the delights of the earth we currently experience.

Hebrews 2:8 clearly implies that in Heaven all things will be subject to humanity. Clearly this first applies to Christ himself, Lord of all,

> "Do we eat food and drink in Heaven?"
>
> Emma, age 5

8. Grudem, *Systematic Theology*, 1161.

but secondarily it is applicable to us as images of Christ and fellow coworkers and heirs. In this sense, we "inherit the earth," a fulfillment of a beatitude promise in Matthew 5:5. What this means is subject to discussion, but it must include bringing order and maintaining it, cultivating beauty, and stewarding God's good creation (Gen 1:31). In fact, we would not be wrong to think that the whole gamut of human enterprise and investigation, human exploration and creativity, human industry and enterprise, will be part of what we will do in the new heavens and earth. I am certainly not alone in thinking this, as we see from this comment from Wayne Grudem: "Perhaps people will work at the whole range of investigation and development of the creation by technological, creative, and inventive means, thus exhibiting the full extent of their excellent creation in the image of God."[9] The next two sections will seek to draw out the implications of what life might be like for us on the new earth.

A final point that has already been mentioned but is worth saying again as I close this section: eternity will be a God-centered life, both literally and relationally. All the images of the new heavens and earth have the triune God at the center of it, and all relating is done in and through and by him. When we come to see and know God face to face, our life shall be complete and our eternal occupation shall be begun. As Bruce Milne has said, "We may be confident that the crowning wonder of our experience in the heavenly realm will be the endless exploration of that unutterable beauty, majesty, love, holiness, power, joy and grace which is God himself."[10]

Let's Talk

Knowing that we will be engaged in various styles of rest and in various forms of activity is one thing; to investigate more deeply what this rest and activity might entail is another. In this section, we tease out the detail of what this new existence might mean for us. In the next section we will examine some of the interesting (and more speculative) questions raised by this material.

We know we shall be eating and drinking, frequenting banquets, and attending parties in eternity (Luke 14:15). Without denying the physical reality of such images, I think we want to inquire a bit deeper into what these mean at a more foundational level. We drink water for survival and

9. Ibid., 1162.

10. Milne, *Know the Truth*, 369.

alcohol (or other non-alcoholic beverages) for social purposes. The same is true with food. We like the taste of drink; it quenches a thirst and complements a meal. We have our favorite foods and many of us enjoy eating cuisine from countries other than our own, discovering new flavors and tastes. Both eating and drinking together provide occasions for deep social interaction with friends and strangers-becoming-friends alike. Eating, drinking, and having parties are all part of being social beings, persons-in-relation, and as such hospitality—hosting and being hosted—is central theological and anthropological act. They are theological because in this way we image God, the Great Host (the one who invites us into his family) and at the same time the Great Guest (the one who was sent from Heaven to earth), and anthropological because they are fundamental to the way God created us (*anthropological* simply means having to do with being human). We have many people through our house and at our table—longtime friends and first-time guests. We won't eat in the new heavens and earth for survival—we will be immortal! We won't eat for sustenance only, although it is not out of the question that we will need to replenish our energy with drink and food after physical activity. We will primarily eat for the joy it brings and the opportunities it affords for participating meaningfully in each other's lives.

Eating together is a key task of what it means to image Christ and it is deeply biblical. Here we might think of the great feasts and meals instituted in the Old Testament, like the Passover meal. Or we could think of when Christ came to earth and ate with people, both the so-called *good* and the so-called *bad*. Mealtimes were an opportunity for deep personal relating. One of my favorite examples is the time when Jesus invited himself to eat at the house of Zacchaeus; by the end of the meal this little man was reborn, renewed, and rejoicing (Luke 19:1–10). Eating on the new earth will be an occasion for fun, for fellowship, and for deeply interpersonal relating. This is part of the reason many of us protect the family mealtime so much.

Will living for eternity in the new heavens and earth be boring? That is the fear of many. One article on Heaven included the author's quip, "Our ancestors were afraid of Hell; we are afraid of Heaven. We think it will be boring."[11] I fail to see how this could ever be the case, but I know, and it was in part the motivation for me writing this book that many struggle to see how exciting the new heavens

"Will we pray in Heaven?"

SUSAN, AGED 9

11. Zaleski, "In Defence of Immortality," 42.

and earth will be for us. So let us tease this issue out and see if we can address it head-on.

Frustration and boredom occur whenever there is an arresting of development at a finite point, whenever one has stopped short of a goal or stopped short of reaching some level of maturity. In the absence of failure or inadequacy, frustration ceases. Hence, life on the new earth will spell the end of *frustration* but certainly not the end of *growth*. We will continue to exercise the perfect character that we will have received from God. John Baille speaks of "development in fruition" as opposed to "development towards fruition."[12] This is a nice distinction and a helpful one. Alexander Maclaren said, "Heaven is endless longing, accompanied with an endless fruition—a longing which is blessedness, a longing which is life!"[13] *Fruition* indicates culmination or completion and fits nicely here: an endlessly culminating fulfillment. Investigation and learning will continue throughout eternity as God's character can never be exhausted, nor the goodness he bestows on his people be fully discovered. And it is this that attracts us to Heaven.

So will an endless duration of time on this new earth be boring? No! Here a distinction made by John Fischer is useful: the distinction between "self-exhausting pleasures" and "repeatable pleasures."[14] A self-exhausting pleasure is one in which once the pleasurable thing is attained, the pleasure is achieved, fulfilled, and is over. To repeat this again (and again, and again) would not be fun. An example of this would be climbing a mountain as part of a larger goal to overcome a fear of heights. Once the goal has been accomplished, the person would have no interest in climbing the mountain again. In fact, to be made to climb the mountain again (and again, and again) would be terrible. Once the fear is overcome, that particular pleasure would be exhausted. Or another example: Our family had the opportunity to go to Disney World in Orlando, Florida. We had three fun-filled days and it was simply incredible. Our children were in the "sweet spot" when it came to their ages and we will cherish memories of this time for as long as we live. But imagine going to Disney World every day, of every year, for your entire

---

12. Baillie, *And the Life Everlasting*, 281. This paragraph is in respectful but direct disagreement with my fellow Baptist theologian Erickson (*Christian Theology*, 1240), who sees no progress on the new earth.

13. Maclaren, "Psalm 42.2, part 3."

14. Fischer, "Why Immortality Is Not So Bad."

lifetime! That would *not* be fun. Disney World is a self-exhausting pleasure (as some of the staff who had to be there every day were clear evidence of).

By contrast, a repeatable pleasure is satisfying for intrinsic reasons and as such is capable of being repeated again and again, for the same or even more levels of enjoyment. Fischer doesn't use this example but, for me, riding a motorcycle (preferably a Harley-Davidson CVO Street Glide Special[15]) would be an infinitely repeatable pleasure. Or think of sports, a fine meal with friends, or appreciating the arts; these are all infinitely repeatable and the pleasure increases rather than being exhausted. In the new heavens and earth pleasures will be infinitely repeatable, distributed in various creative patterns so that we will never tire of enjoying them. In the words of two Baptist theologians, "Think of the most joy-filled moments in your life. Subtract the sadness that comes when we realize how fleeting our temporal pleasures are. Add the immediate presence of God. Multiply by infinity, and that yields something of what heaven will be like!"[16]

Memories, I believe, are often a repeatable pleasure. Whatever else eternity means, surely it involves a never-ending supply of good memories: good memory piled upon good memory. A really fun and enjoyable moment becomes a memory that gets better and more pleasurable over time. Remember the first time you saw your spouse? How precious is that memory now, many years later, as you have come to know your spouse better than any other person you have ever met? Or think back to the first time you heard your unborn child's heartbeat or felt them kick or squirm. Oh wow! I cried at the first sonogram my wife had and now, years later, that memory still makes me smile, and sometimes cry a little. Or I think back to when my daughter was born. She wasn't breathing and she was red like a yam (red and bumpy for those who don't know what yams are). (My wife tells me Sydney was actually purple; I am color blind after all!) They put Sydney on oxygen and held her upright and I saw the color flush out of her as she took her first deep breath and then . . . let out a cry—a cry of life! Seeing her now, I can still see her then and the memory gets more exquisite each time. We often think an experience and its memory are different things. They are not. C. S. Lewis taught me this. In his Cosmic Trilogy written for adults, which I love, he has Ransom, a space-traveling man, meet an alien, a *hross* named Hyoi, on the planet of Malacandra (Mars). Hyoi teaches Ransom that "A

---

15. I do hope my family and friends are getting the hint!

16. Lewis and Demarest, *Integrative Theology*, 3:480.

pleasure is full grown only when it is remembered."[17] That is why we take photos and video of our favorite moments: to "capture" them to enjoy again and again. We can't imagine a hard drive big enough to store all the good memories we are going to have in the new heavens and earth.

In a work on George MacDonald, Scottish author and minister (and a literary influence on C. S. Lewis and J. R. R. Tolkien) Gordon Reid noted one of the central convictions behind his fantasy novels.

> It is true also that the vast majority of ordinary Christians, while no doubt impassively acquiescing in the idea of heaven, find it difficult to summon up any enthusiasm for the place. The images of jewelled cities and thrones, of golden crowns and crystal seas, of harps and incense, leave them cold. How much more attractive the (equally metaphorical) visions of some modern science fiction: exciting—and dangerous—explorations of new worlds' long, patient years of living with and understanding other races of beings; comradeship and love winning through against malice and evil. That's closer to a heaven worth aiming for—not a boring place of eternal rest and peace, but a vibrant life of love and service.
>
> And that is exactly George MacDonald's view of life after death. The idea of a static place or condition of peace and rest had little attraction for him. . . . Macdonald's vision of life after death is much more dynamic and moving. . . .
>
> Then the adventure would begin; then real life, as it is meant to be lived, would flow on through eternity, not changeless or boring, but life that would develop and expand in excitement and beauty and love, in a way that is only hinted at in this present life. But these hints of the true life are the most valuable moments in anyone's life . . .[18]

"Are there animals in Heaven?"

EMMA, AGE 6

I have already made the case that there will be unending progress in the resurrection, morally, spiritually, intellectually, and physically. As God is supremely infinite and beyond all our comprehension, we can be assured that there are aspects to God that we have never seen, felt, or experienced, and we will spend an eternity discovering what he has yet to reveal about himself to us, not to mention what he has yet to reveal of his new creation. This will be an ever-deepening relationship of

17. Lewis, *Out of the Silent Planet*, 89.
18. Reid, "Afterword."

love and will be *the* life worth living (to answer Socrates' question, "What would a life worth living look like?"). There will be a necessary social dimension to this as well, as we work with others to grow and mature in our endless love, admiration, and appreciation of the divine nature seen in the Father, Son, and Holy Spirit. Randy Alcorn has one suggestion for why some Christians think the new earth could be boring when he writes, "Our belief that Heaven will be boring betrays a heresy—that God is boring." He continues, "There's no greater nonsense."[19] He is right, of course! If worship (in the fullest sense of the term) is boring here on earth, you are in for a hard time in the new heavens and earth.

The concept of progress in Heaven is worth dwelling on further. Imagine playing golf on the new earth (and why wouldn't there be golf?). We won't be hitting hole-in-one's with our eyes closed. Or imagine making a jigsaw puzzle (and why wouldn't there be jigsaw puzzles?). We won't be putting them together with one hand behind our backs and looking the other way. Or for the builders and woodworkers out there; the craftsmanship, the labor, and the learned skills will all need to be acquired, honed, and practiced in order to make useful and beautiful things. Or the artists; the technique, the eye, and understanding of composition will all be required to create great art, and that will take time, skill, and patience. Or our gardeners; throw a bag of mixed seeds on an empty plot and come back in the afternoon to see an immaculately designed and tended garden? No! Landscape artists and others will still be required, to give advice, to plan, and to trial designs, test plant suitability, and so forth. And as the garden is tended and looked after, the plants will grow and mature, without thistles and thorns to ruin it, into a splendid (or not so splendid) garden of your own design. The new heavens and earth are just as much a place of purpose as life on this earth is now. So let us not stop thinking about plans, designs, creativity, and intellectual effort; these are all good gifts that will be used in the future.

In 1 Corinthians 13:13 Paul makes one of his now-famous sayings, "And now these three remain: faith, hope and love. But the greatest of these is love." Every year I ask my students the following question, and now I ask it of you: "We can easily think of how faith remains for all eternity—we will always believe in and trust in the Father of our Lord Jesus Christ. We can easily think of how love remains for all eternity—we will always love the triune God of grace and glory. But how are we to think of hope remaining

19. Alcorn, *Heaven*, 410.

for all eternity?" I paraphrase this verse as follows: "These three remain: faith, hope, and love. But the most ambiguous is hope." My question stumps 98 percent (I made that figure up) of my students. How did you do? In light of the biblical notion of progress into eternity, I hope you were able to make an initial reply. A biblical definition of hope is having a confident expectation that what is not currently a reality one day will be. It is not based on wishful thinking ("I hope the children have a nice day at school today"), nor is it based upon the efforts of a finite fellow-human ("I hope Mummy earns enough for us to have a holiday this year"). Rather, Christian hope is founded upon our unchanging God and his never-failing Word. As the old hymn by Edward Mote has it:

> My hope is built on nothing less
> Than Jesus' blood and righteousness;
> I dare not trust the sweetest frame,
> But wholly lean on Jesus' name.
> On Christ, the solid Rock, I stand;
> All other ground is sinking sand.

Hope into eternity will look like progress, growth, and achievement. As we continue to chase after God's being, goodness, and presence, there will always be more to come and so much more to hope for. As one thing is hoped for and then achieved, another will present itself. Mostly, we will never outstrip the Father's knowledge, never exhaust the Son's love, never tire of the Spirit's presence, and never reach the end of God's creation. This is a thrilling notion and is but another reason why eternal life with God in the new heavens and earth cannot and will not be boring. We join with the psalmist in proclaiming, "In your presence there is fullness of joy; at your right hand are pleasures forevermore" (Ps 16:11).

For many people hearing this for the first time, a notion occurs to them: namely, aren't we perfect after the resurrection? We tend to immediately think perfection is static, and that is boring. But perfection does not have to mean static at all, and it certainly doesn't carry that connotation in Scripture. Hebrews speaks a lot about perfection (Heb 12:22–23 for instance). We could contrast perfection with rest: rest from enemies, from sin, and from the struggle of fallenness. Perfection, then, is to be in a kind of Sabbath state, the state that most closely approximates play. Not "kids' play," but more the sort of play that a scientist does in the lab, or an inventor does in her garage, or a parent does on a rainy weekend with her young children—inventive play, creative play, educational play, stimulating play, productive play; that sort of play. It is the sort of play that we see God doing each day, which can look to us like work but, with the right lenses on, is really seen as godly play. Here I am thinking of the sunrise (I know the sun does not actually rise, but bear with me). We know scientifically what is happening here, about planetary revolutions and so on. But don't let us fool ourselves into thinking God has established the so-called laws of nature and now just sits back and watches. That would be a form of deism, of a disinterested and uninvolved god, not the God of Scripture who is constantly and continuously involved in his creation as the Son sustains the world and the Spirit brings it to perfection as the Father wills. Seen from this vantage point, this insider's view, if you will, each sunrise is a miracle, a work of God that he does tirelessly, day after day, for our delight and for his glory. That is the sort of play I am talking about; godly play is godly work when you are perfect and living in a perfect world. It is fun, it is stimulating, it is rewarding, it is useful, it is creative, it is faithful, and it is God-honoring.

Another feature of life on the new earth is the diversity of people there. The population of the new earth will be made up of a vast array of cultures, ethnicities, languages, tribes, and people. "After this I looked, and there before me was a great multitude that no one could count, from every nation, tribe, people and language, standing before the throne and before the Lamb. They were wearing white robes and were holding palm branches in their hands" (Rev 7:9). What each will have in common is Christ and the gospel. The community of the new earth will be truly multicultural. Revelation 21:3 has an interesting and important teaching buried within it: "And I heard a loud voice from the throne saying, 'Behold, the dwelling place of God is with man. He will dwell with them, and they will be his *peoples*, and God himself will be with them as their God.'" Notice that it says God will be with his *peoples*—plural. We see here a fulfillment of what was promised earlier in Isaiah 25, where God promised to prepare a feast at the end times on Mount Zion for "all peoples." Revelation 21:24 reminds us that not only will people from every nation, tribe, and tongue be present on the new earth, but they will take redeemed aspects of their cultures with them: "The nations will walk by its light, and the kings of the earth will bring their splendor into it." Nothing of worth that has begun on earth will fail to make an appearance on the new earth. What God has begun now he will continue to perfect then. Bruce Milne helpfully reminds us that "Everything which authentically reflects the God of truth, all that is of abiding worth from within the national stories and the cultural inheritance of the world's peoples, will find its place in the New Jerusalem."[20]

Working within a multicultural context in New Zealand, I am often confronted with questions from students such as, "Can I be Samoan *and* Christian?" Or, "Do I have to give up my cultural identity as Māori in order to embrace the Gospel of Jesus Christ?" This and other verses in Holy Scripture teach us that we don't have to give up our cultural and ethnic identity in order to be like Christ. Instead, God redeems all cultures and makes them fit for the new heavens and earth. My daughter is part of her school's kapa haka group (a Māori performance group). Although she is of European descent (Dutch on her father's side and Scottish on her mother's side), Sydney loves to participate in another culture—to sing their songs, learn their dances, and appreciate their ways of being. There is no reason to think she won't be in a kapa haka group on the new earth as well.[21]

One of the ways we image Jesus Christ in our humanity is through the cultivation of culture. We are tasked with bringing all creation under God's rule and presenting it to him in an act of worship. Life in the new heavens and earth will be no different, except sin and folly will no longer be our constant companions. Life in eternity will be full of creative expression in the arts, sciences, sports and recreation, and all of life. As created co-creators with God, we will be given a vast canvas to work on, increased levels of skillfulness to draw on, and a collaborative environment to work within. The imagination is our only barrier to what we might accomplish in this renewed world.

Life on the new earth will be indelibly social. Ed Strauss suggests that when we get to Heaven we might like to spend time talking to the great heroes of the faith (Matt 8:11). He offers the following questions, which might be fun to talk over with our kids:

- "Ask Noah how he built such a huge ship and if all those animals got along together.

- Ask Moses what it was like to split the sea wide open so people could walk through it.

20. Milne, *Message of Heaven and Hell*, 321.

21. Māori are the indigenous population of New Zealand and *Kapa haka* is the term for Māori performing arts, and literally means to form a line (*kapa*) and dance (*haka*). It involves an emotional and powerful combination of song, dance, and Māori language. *Kapa haka* is performed by cultural groups on marae, at schools, and during special events and festivals.

- Ask Joshua what it sounded like when the walls of Jericho fell down.

- Ask Joseph how it felt to be picked on by his brothers and then, later, rule over all of Egypt.

- Ask David if he felt afraid to fight the scary giant, Goliath.

- Ask Peter how it felt when he walked on water."[22]

Do you like the earth? Then you are going to love Heaven! Do you enjoy earthly delights—like ripe tomatoes, fresh strawberries, feijoas from the tree, the feel of sand between your toes as you walk along the beach, seeing a rainbow break through a cloudy sky, the smell of a newborn, the anticipation of Christmas Eve, losing yourself in a dance or a song? Then remember where such gifts come from: God, who through Christ and by the Spirit invented all the pleasures of creation. Every taste, smell, sight, and sense was his extravagant idea. And that same creative triune God is right now, preparing a place for us to inhabit for all eternity.

> "Is there still 'time out' in Heaven?"
>
> MICAH, AGE 5

Let's Play

We have covered a lot of ground already regarding what we might be doing on the new earth, and we have entertained some possible implications of the biblical teaching we are given. In this final section, we simply want to play with some of these concepts and images a bit more, looking for ways we might engage our children's imagination, baptizing it in scriptural echoes.

We now know that every holy aspect of human culture will flourish in the new heavens and earth, and that will make us incredibly and wonderfully engaged in a vast array of endeavors. Coming from a working-class background, I was encouraged into a trade at high school, so I took classes in woodwork, metalwork, technical graphics, and the like. I was, to put it mildly, useless. I am practically incompetent; the spirit is willing but the body doesn't seem to agree. I can labor, but *skilled* labor—that is another thing. Imagine what I will be able to do on the new earth, though! I will be able to be apprenticed by a master builder, spend time in the garage with an excellent wood turner, accompany and be trained by an artist, and practice

22. Strauss, *Heaven for Kids*, 61.

and be mentored by the best artisans in the world. It will take time, effort, and trial and error, but I will eventually be able to make things that are both useful and beautiful. I might not ever be as good as the master artisans (in fact, I won't ever be as good as them), but I could be satisfied. The same goes for music. I am tone deaf and can't keep a beat (you might be working out why I am a theologian—I can't do anything else!). But on the new earth I truly believe I will be able to learn to play the guitar and play riffs from my favorite Mark Knopfler tunes. I won't ever be as good as Knopfler, but I will be satisfied; and at a minimum I will be able to sing in tune (you don't know how glad my family is to hear this).

Here on earth, I worship God as best I can. I pray regularly, read God's Holy Word, attend and serve at church, and try to lead a godly life. But sin gets in the way: my sin, your sin, and sin in general (which we normally call evil). With Paul I can truly say:

> I do not understand what I do. For what I want to do I do not do, but what I hate I do. And if I do what I do not want to do, I agree that the law is good. As it is, it is no longer I myself who do it, but it is sin living in me. For I know that good itself does not dwell in me, that is, in my sinful nature. For I have the desire to do what is good, but I cannot carry it out. For I do not do the good I want to do, but the evil I do not want to do—this I keep on doing. Now if I do what I do not want to do, it is no longer I who do it, but it is sin living in me that does it. (Rom 7:15–20)

That is not the whole story of course, as Paul goes on to say in Romans 8:1–4:

> Therefore, there is now no condemnation for those who are in Christ Jesus, because through Christ Jesus the law of the Spirit who gives life has set you free from the law of sin and death. For what the law was powerless to do because it was weakened by the flesh, God did by sending his own Son in the likeness of sinful flesh to be a sin offering. And so he condemned sin in the flesh, in order that the righteous requirement of the law might be fully met in us, who do not live according to the flesh but according to the Spirit.

But think of resurrection life in the new heavens and earth. No more sin, no more struggle to be holy, no more resistance. There we will be wholly committed to the will of God and we will be able to bring the Father glory by perfect obedience, bring the Son glory through perfect love, and bring the Spirit glory through perfect fellowship. All our impulses will be godly, all our desires will be holy, and all our energy will be spent in joyful God-honoring activity. Welcomed by the Father with the words "good and faithful servant," we shall continue to hear the Master's voice delight in our thoughts, motives, and actions. I can't wait. The utter peace and *rest* this suggests is almost overwhelming.

This nearly overwhelming sense of what is in store for us is beautifully depicted by C. S. Lewis in his little essay "The Weight of Glory." Taking with full seriousness the biblical teaching on rewards that await the faithful follower of Jesus Christ, Lewis concludes:

> . . . it would seem that Our Lord finds our desires, not too strong, but too weak. We are half-hearted creatures, fooling about with drink and sex and ambition when an infinite joy is offered us, like an ignorant child who wants to go on making mud pies in a slum because he cannot imagine what is meant by the offer of a holiday at the sea. We are far too easily pleased.[23]

The rewards we are promised, as we have seen earlier, "are not tacked on to the activity for which they are given," Lewis reminds us, "but are the activity itself in consummation."[24] We have seen this already when we concluded that rewards in Heaven had to be opportunities for greater service. But Lewis reminds us that only those who have achieved such rewards fully know this. Lewis asks us to think of reading. The adult knows that books open up entire worlds within which we can lose ourselves. Reading is a pure delight for many of us, myself included, and so we read short stories from Enid Blyton or epics from Leo Tolstoy, fiction from Wendell Berry, and non-fiction from Maya Angelou. But to the elementary school student just starting out, who knows nothing of this delight, they have to be taught the alphabet and then grammar and so to read. But teaching them will involve hard work, discipline, and the promise of rewards. Rewards for them may take the form of gold stars, small prizes from their teacher, or gifts from parents. At some point, though, the offer of lesser rewards gives way to the reward itself; the joy of reading is gift enough. It is the same in the Christian life. We often have to offer our children lesser incentives to be good, to worship God, and to live a godly life, all the while training them up in the ways and knowledge of God until they love him with all their

23. Lewis, "Weight of Glory," 94–95.
24. Ibid., 95.

heart and serve him with all their strength simply for the joy that loving and serving God brings.

> The Christian, in relation to heaven, is in much the same position as the schoolboy. Those who have attained everlasting life in the vision of God doubtless know very well that it is no mere bribe, but the very consummation of their earthly discipleship; but we who have not yet attained it cannot know this in the same way, and cannot even begin to know it at all except by continuing to obey and finding the first reward of our obedience in our increasing power to desire the ultimate reward. . . . Poetry replaces grammar, gospel replaces law, longing transforms obedience, as gradually as the tide lifts a grounded ship.[25]

Lewis notes a key difference between learning to read with the Christian hope of eternal life: the difference is that God has made us for the new heavens and earth and so he has placed a proper desire for himself within us (remember that saying from Augustine earlier?). This is what I would suggest you tease out with your children. What desires do they have and how can they be seen as God-given capacities for eternal life? What do I mean? My son, Liam, loves to create stories and tell them to us. They are short stories, admittedly, but he constantly paints scenarios with characters and a plot. More often than not his stories are incredibly funny. I might ask him where all this creativity comes from and point him to the ultimate Creator, God the Father, Son, and Holy Spirit. Once that link *back* to creation has been made, I might then turn his thoughts *forward* to where such creativity will finally be unleashed and unbounded in the new heavens and earth, for God's greater glory.

I want to press this point home even more. Some of you reading this book will be lawyers, others stay-at-home parents, and others still may be nurses, teachers, engineers, laborers, plumbers, or artists. If this is a job you have chosen, and one in which you find a good deal of joy (despite the trials that necessarily come with all jobs), then to you too I would ask the same questions. Where did the lawyer's joy in bringing order out of chaos come from? Here I would point you *back* to creation and how the triune God created all things, before turning your thoughts *forward* to eternity. What might our lawyers be doing in eternity? They won't be litigating! But it is possible they will still be using their God-given talents in administration, in judging (without conflict), and in bringing further order to what is already

25. Ibid., 96.

ordered. Or what will God have in store for accountants? What will they be calculating, counting, and balancing, I wonder? You see, whatever the passion, whatever the talent, God will redeem it and use it and enable you to use that for his praise and for your enjoyment. As we shepherd children into educational programs and give them career advice, perhaps a vision of the new heavens and earth might be a help to us and to them.

Remaining with Lewis, he reminds us that the idea of *glory* is prominent in biblical portrayals of eternity. Glory carries two senses in Scripture: fame and luminosity. In regards to fame, this is not the fame conferred by fellow creatures but fame with God—approval or even, dare we say, appreciation by God. This is what I was getting at earlier when I mentioned how we look forward to hearing God say to us, "Well done, good and faithful servant." This is not some vainglory longing. Lewis came to this conclusion as well. "I suddenly remembered that no one can enter heaven except as a child; and nothing is so obvious in a child—not in a conceited child, but in a good child—as its great and undisguised pleasure in being praised."[26] What a motivation for service, to know that the one whom we love more than anything else in the world might be pleased with us, might enjoy our company, and might pat us on the back. This is not vanity; it is the recognition that God alone is good (Mark 10:18) and what *he* calls good is good indeed. If God is satisfied with our work, then how much more shall we be satisfied with ourselves? Here is the basis for good self-image. Lewis concludes this line of thought with these stunning words:

> The promise of glory is the promise, almost incredible and only possible by the work of Christ, that some of us, that any of us who really chooses, shall actually survive the examination, shall find approval, shall please God. To please God . . . to be a real ingredient in the divine happiness . . . to be loved by God, not merely pitied, but delighted in as an artist delights in his work or a father in a son—it seems impossible, a weight or burden of glory which our thoughts can hardly sustain. But so it is.[27]

What will we be doing in the new heavens and earth? We will be resting and we will be working; we will be creating and we will be playing. With all of the creation we will be worshipping God by doing that for which we were created. I conclude this chapter with a summary of what we will be doing from Richard Middleton.

26. Ibid., 100.
27. Ibid., 104.

In the biblical worldview mountains and stars worship God just as much as humans do . . . (Ps 148). . . . But how do mountains and stars worship God? Certainly not verbally or with emotions. Rather, mountains worship God simply by being mountains . . . And Stars worship God by being stars. . . . If mountains worship God by being mountains and stars worship God by being stars how do humans worship God? By being human, in the full glory of what that means. Humans, the Bible tells us, are cultural beings, defined not by our worship, for worship is what defines creation (all creatures are called to worship). But the human creature is made to worship God in a distinctive way: by interacting with the earth, using our God-given power to transform our earthly environment into a complex world (a sociocultural world) that glorifies the creator.[28]

Summary

In this chapter I have tried to communicate the following:

- Our promised "rest" will be rest from enemies, from sin, and from all that could separate us from God.

- Life in the new heavens and earth will be characterized by times of refreshing delight.

- Active worship forms the heart of our activity in the New Jerusalem.

- We were created for a lifetime of soul-enriching work in God's city.

- We shall rule with Christ and we shall reign with Christ.

- We will be eating, drinking, resting, working, exploring, playing, learning, growing, maturing, hosting, and visiting.

- Godly play, like inventing, creating, and working, will occupy our lives.

- We can think of no place more exciting than the New Jerusalem.

28. Middleton, *New Heaven and a New Earth*, 41.

Chapter 5

A Great Cloud of Witnesses
(Who Will Be in Zion?)

If I ever reach heaven I expect to find three wonders there, first, to meet some I had not thought to see there; second, to miss some I had expected to see there; and third, the greatest wonder of all, to find myself there.[1]

JOHN NEWTON

It was a glorious resurrection-morning. The night had been spent in preparing it! The children went gamboling before, and the beasts came after us. Fluttering butterflies, darting dragon-flies hovered or shot hither and thither about our heads, a cloud of colours and flashes, now descending upon us like a snow-storm of rainbow flakes, now rising into the humid air like a rolling vapour of embodied odours. It was a summer-day more like itself, that is, more ideal, than ever man that had not died found summer-day in any world. I walked on the new earth, under the new heaven, and found them the same as the old, save that now they opened their minds to me, and I saw into them. Now, the soul of everything I met came out to greet me and make friends with me, telling me we came from the same, and meant the same.[2]

MR. VANE, IN *LILITH*

1. While I can find no specific reference to this citation in Newton's works, it is commonly ascribed to Newton and certainly sounds like something he would have said.

2. MacDonald, *Lilith*, ch. 45.

Even though most of the heavy lifting has been done already in regards to what the new heavens and earth will be like and what we will do there, this chapter provides some resources for one additional set of questions many will ask and children will need to be taught answers to: Who will and won't be in Zion (the heavenly city or city of God, Heb 12:22)? In this chapter I want to address three questions: How do we know we will be there? Are we sure some people won't be there? Finally, what about animals, specifically our pets; will any of them be there? Some of these questions are central while others appear trivial, and yet for children it is not clear which is which. Some of these questions are clearly addressed in Holy Scripture and can be categorically answered; others will have to be answered tentatively and held to lightly.

Let's Listen

If we ask who is in Zion we have to answer that God is, angels are, believers are, and animals are. This we know from Holy Scripture and we have commented on aspects of this already. But when we take a deeper look at the questions more detail and texture is evident.

No discussion of Zion would be complete without some mention of God's angelic host. Countless numbers of Christians in the East and West alike have affirmed throughout the centuries, "We believe in God the Father, maker of heaven and earth, and of all things visible and invisible" (the Nicene Creed). Part of that invisible world is that of spiritual beings, created by God for his purposes.

Angels are mentioned almost three hundred times in Scripture and are only noticeably absent from books such as Ruth, Nehemiah, Esther, the letters of John, and James. The word *angel* comes from the Hebrew *mal'ak* and the Greek *angelos*, which literally means "messenger," or an ambassador in human affairs, one who speaks or acts in the place of the one who has sent him. According to Nehemiah 9:6 and Psalm 148:2–5, angels were created by God. When we add the New Testament testimony of this, with Paul saying in Colossians 1:16 that God created all things "visible and invisible" through Christ and for him, and then specifically including the angelic world with the phrase, "whether thrones or dominions or principalities or authorities," we can be sure that angels are not independent of God; he created them and so they had a beginning. Hebrews 1:14 reads, "Are not all angels ministering spirits sent to serve those who will inherit salvation?" This tells us that angels do not have bodies like us; they are spirits or spiritual creatures that cannot normally be seen by us unless God gives us special ability to see them (Num 22:31; 2 Kgs 6:17; Luke 2:13). From time to time God allows an angel to take on a human form and be visible to us (Matt 28:5; Heb 13:2). This is rare in Scripture, though.

Angels are spiritual beings created by God to serve him and to do his will. Angels, as created beings, are limited in knowledge and location; they only know what they are taught or learn (they are not omniscient—all-knowing), and they are certainly not omnipresent (all-present). They are glorious creatures, but creatures nonetheless (1 Tim 5:21).

Angels come in an array of types, it would seem. We can speak of three broad categories of angelical beings: cherubim, seraphim, and the unusual living creatures. *Cherubim* (the word means "to till or plough," and is expressive of diligent service) guarded the entrance to the garden of Eden (Gen 3:24), and they are often linked to the throne of God or described as forming his chariot (Ps 18:10; Ezek 10:1–22). Cherubim designs were incorporated into the walls of the sanctuary (Ezek 41:18–25) and the veil of the tabernacle (Exod 26:31). Solomon placed two wooden cherubim plated with gold leaf in the most holy place of the temple, looking toward the holy place. They stood ten cubits (about fourteen feet) high and their wings were five cubits (about seven feet) long.

The second group of angels are the seraphim. *Seraphim* means "burners" or "burning ones," indicating their ardent love and flaming zeal for the honor and service of their Creator, and are only mentioned in Isaiah 6:2–7. They continually worship the Lord and call to one another, "Holy, holy, holy is the Lord of hosts."

The third group of angels are the living creatures spoken of in Ezekiel 1:5–14 and Revelation 4:6–8. These angels have four faces: those of a man, a lion, a bull, and an eagle; and they worship God continually. The four faces are thought by many to represent the entirety of God's creation, making these angels incredibly important.

Angels are organized, it would appear from Holy Scripture, into hierarchies and orders. Daniel 10:13; 1 Thesselonians 4:16; Jude 9; and Revelation 12:7–8 all indicate some form of levels of rank for angels, from Michael, the "archangel" and general of an angelic army, to Gabriel (Dan 8:15–17; 9:21–23; Luke 1:8–38), a bearer of God's most special messages.

In addition to these special categories of angels, we know from God's Word that there is a great army of angels (Deut 33:2; Ps 68:17). Hebrews

12:22 says there are "innumerable angels" and in Revelation 5:11 we are told the angels number "thousands upon thousands, and ten thousand times ten thousand." Clearly, Scripture indicates that there are uncountable numbers of angels in existence (but not an infinite number; the point is, only God knows how many there are). Many of the great thinkers in Christian history held that the ratio between the number of angels and that of all human beings past, present, and future is ninety-nine to one. Their theory was that the lost sheep of the gospel parable represent humanity and the ninety and nine faithful good sheep the good angels. While we know this theory is wrong, the actual number of the angels may be closer to the truth than we think.

The 273 references in the Bible to angels are largely accounts of their activities, and by these a very wide area of ministry is opened up to us. Angels carry messages from God (Luke 1:11–19; Acts 8:26), they praise God for who he is and what he has done (Ps 103:20; Isa 6:2–3), they guide and assist humans in serving God (Dan 6:22; Acts 5:19–20), they protect people, they fight spiritual battles with demons (Dan 10:13; Rev 12:7–8), and they do God's bidding (2 Sam 24:16–17; Acts 12:23).

In addition to good or elect angels, there are fallen angels, more commonly known as demons. The New Testament and the Old Testament (Deut 32:17; Ps 106:37; Judg 9:23–24; 1 Sam 16:15–16) together are very clear that demons exist. These too have their hierarchies, which we can identify as Satan, demons, principalities, and powers. Fallen angels (demons) were created good but rebelled when given the chance, and their judgment is irreversible. *Demon* or *devil* is from the Greek *daimonic* and *daimonion*, the regular terms in the Gospels for the spiritual beings corrupt and hostile to both God and humanity.

On the basis of texts such as Isaiah 14:12–15; Ezekiel 28:1–11; Matthew 12:24; 17:18; and Ephesians 3:10; 6:12, we can see that Satan is the prince of the demons, indicating that since their leader is an angel the demons must also be angels, but fallen as Satan is. We also know that Satan has well-organized ranks of angels who further his purposes. This indicates that the same kinds of beings make up the personnel of these ranks as do the angels (from the Ephesians passages) and therefore that evil beings are fallen angels. Finally, we can see that the demons are not human but spirits. In conclusion, we must say that nowhere in Scripture are demons directly said to be *fallen angels*, but the evidence just cited would seem to point to the conclusion that they are. Although demons have a measure of freedom in worldly affairs now, they will eventually all be confined to Hell (2 Pet 2:4; Jude 6). Satan is an evil, arrogant, proud, and nasty fallen angel. But he is just that—a fallen angel. He is not all-powerful, all-knowing, or all-mighty. He is a localized being, which means he can only be in one place at one time, and he is a creature, thus he comes well short of the glory of God. We must keep this in mind.

We will look more closely at what angels do in Zion and affirm their presence there, whilst also confirming the absence of demons in Zion. Although very different from humans, angels will be our fellow heavenly citizens.

With angels, we know there will be humans in Zion. From all that we have examined so far in this book it is clear that Zion is for Christians, those savingly united to Jesus Christ. The only people who get into Zion are resurrected children of God. For this reason, we can affirm the fact that Zion is redemptive, fixed, and final, to use Paul Helm's terms. Eternal life with the triune God in Zion is redemptive because no one goes there by default. God is clear in his Word that sin is what separates us from him (Rom 3:23) and it is only by the grace of the Lord Jesus Christ and the fellowship of the Holy Spirit that we can be right with God and have Zion as our eternal home (Matt 7:13–14). The new heavens and earth are the home God originally intended for all his creatures. Unfortunately, with Adam and Eve sin entered the world and with it the alienating effects of a life lived apart from God. But God's plans will not be thwarted and so he has made a way for all people to again be right with him and made fit for Zion. Through the life, death, and resurrection of Jesus Christ all people will gain immortality, some to an immortal life and some to an immortal death. Immortal life means life with God in Zion. Immortal death means the opposite: to live forever (immortality) without the presence of God to bless (a living death). There is no prospect of Zion without Christ. "So heaven is made possible—and made actual for believers—by the work of Christ, and by his work alone. Heaven is the crown of salvation, the ultimate blessing."[3] This explains why the new heavens and earth are utterly Christ-centered. Christ is the heart of Zion, the one who gives it meaning (Rev 21:23).

Zion is also fixed and final. This is the opposite of what life on earth is like. Here and now everything is in flux; it is all up for grabs. We never know if a loved one will make it home from a journey without being involved in

---

3. Helm, *Last Things*, 90.

an automobile accident, or if cancer will strike an otherwise healthy friend. But in the new heavens and earth there is a security that is final and fixed for all time. Resurrection means a life that will not suffer, and could never turn from God. Our existence in Zion will be fixed because once there we will never want to leave and we never can leave. The only other place to go would be Hell and that is not an option. We make our choices in this life, not the next. It is also impossible in Zion to sin; we will have new natures and new bodies, like Christ's, to live as he does. Paul Helm reminds us that "heaven is static to the extent that the moral character of believers in heaven can never decay. There will be growth and movement in heaven, no doubt, because there cannot be bodies without change, but there will be no decay."[4]

Given the fact that many people are not believers, we can rightly conclude that there will be many people who will not inherit the earth (Eph 2:12). Such people, unfortunately, go to Hell and are eternally separated from the presence of God to bless (Matt 8:12). The focus of this book is the new heavens and earth, but some brief comment on Hell is required. As with believers, unbelievers will also be resurrected to eternal life (Matt 25:46). Like believers, unbelievers will also be judged for the things done in the body (Rev 20:11–15). The basis of judgment will be the same: Have people responded to divine grace with faith and then lived a life of good works? For those whose foundation is not Jesus Christ, those who have no faith in Christ or filling of the Holy Spirit, God says their names are not written in the Lamb's book of life and, as such, they cannot enter the new heavens and earth (Rev 20:12). Upon judgment of their life they will be consigned to Hell, that place God created for fallen angels (demons) (Matt 25:41). The great tragedy is that humans will occupy a place God intended for Satan and his host. Those not savingly united to Christ will not be fellow citizens of Zion.

Hell is variously described in Scripture as a "fire" (Matt 25:41), a state of "outer darkness" (Matt 8:12), "eternal punishment" (Matt 25:46), "torment" (Rev 14:10–11), a "bottomless pit" (Rev 9:1–2,11), the "wrath of God" (Rom 2:5), a "second death" (Rev 21:8), "eternal destruction," and "exclusion from the face of the Lord" (2 Thess 1:9). Hell is characterized as misery, loneliness, a realization that Christ is Lord of all and then being cut off from him. It is an eternal, conscious existence and is morally and

4. Ibid., 91.

spiritually permanent, thus it is a hopeless condition. Hell is an awful topic, but one Jesus and his followers were careful to warn us about. I mention the reality of Hell here as in the next two sections we will have to draw a few contrasts between those who are in the new heaven and earth and those who are not. Naturally, if people are not in Zion we want to know where they are.

When it comes to the question of who will be in Zion, our children will almost always ask us if animals will be there with us. But this is often a question hidden within a question. The real question they are asking is this: Will any of our pets be there? We shall have a lot more to say about this in the next two sections, but for now it will be enough to say that we have already affirmed the fact that in the new heavens and earth there will be a great number and variety of animals present. I have already tipped my hat to the fact that I think there will be a greater variety of animals there than any of us have ever experienced here on this present earth. The question of pets in Zion is a good one, but it is one that can only be given an approximate answer based on what we know to be otherwise true.

The population of Zion will consist of the triune God, his heavenly host of angels, believers of all times and places, and a vast array of animal life. These will be our eternal companions. Let's talk about this population more in the next section before playing with some of these themes as we conclude this chapter.

Let's Talk

Given the reality that Zion is redemptive, fixed, and final, what does this mean for us? In the first instance, it surely means we have to communicate to our children (and learn the lesson ourselves of course) that the most important thing in life is a relationship with God, in which we love him above all else and serve him before all else. Responding to God's grace in faith and then seeking to live a holy life will ensure we know where our eternal home is and whom it is with. That is the first thing. To be assured of salvation and then assured of our resurrection is vital. In 1 Corithians 15:14 Paul clearly tells us that "if Christ has not been raised, our preaching is useless and so is your faith." Only after knowing of our salvation by grace through faith, and our future bodily resurrection to be with Christ, can we really talk about what eternal life will look like and feel like.

We have already seen that in the resurrection we will have new natures, renewed bodies, and new abilities. This means that our fellow neighbors in Zion will be like Jesus and so like us; they will be morally pure, physically healthy, and emotionally mature. Our fellow citizens will be fit for the new heavens and earth in every possible way (". . . it will be raised a spiritual body," 1 Cor 15:44). In other words, we will be truly free for the first time in the resurrection. This freedom, according to biblical Christianity, involves the inability to sin. If we define sin as thinking, feeling, or doing anything contrary to the glory of God, then in the resurrection we will be unable to sin.

Many people struggle with this idea as they have unwittingly accepted a secular notion of what freedom is. For many, freedom is the ability to make a decision between two or more alternatives without *any* determining factors other than free will to choose from a list of options. This is not a Christian view of freedom. Only God is truly free. And God cannot sin; he cannot do what is contrary to his nature, for his actions and his nature are the same thing. Let me explain. God loves because God is love. If Jesus is God (and he is), then Jesus can't sin. Jesus can't do that which brings dishonor to God, he can't do anything that is contrary to the will of God, and he can't live a life, even for a second, that is opposed to God—for he is God. However, if Jesus is human (and he is), then his life is the model for our own. Like Jesus, we are only truly free when all we desire, and will, and do is for God's glory and fame. In short, Jesus didn't sin because he couldn't sin, and he couldn't sin because he didn't want to sin, and he didn't want to sin because his entire being was directed to the love of God (whether or not Jesus knew he couldn't sin is a question best left for another time).[5] In the resurrection, we too will be like Christ. We too will have new natures and new bodies, a renewed will and a renewed heart; to follow God, to love God, and to glorify him forever. In the resurrection we can't sin because we won't want to sin.

"Will people annoy us in Heaven?"

ROGER, AGE 8

Biblical freedom is the freedom to obey, not the freedom to choose to disobey. Having the freedom to disobey and to sin is a condition of the fall; it has more to do with being in bondage to sin that it does with being free for God. There will be nothing in our resurrected bodies or in the new

5. I have addressed this question directly elsewhere. See Habets, *Anointed Son*, 139–44; 263–67.

heavens and earth that will ever make us want to sin. "The freedom of heaven, then, is the freedom from sin; not that the believer just happens to be free from sin, but that he is so constituted or reconstituted that he *cannot* sin. He does not want to sin, and he does not want to want to sin. And in this respect he is like Christ, who, though tempted, yet could not sin."[6] Citizens of Zion will be a delight to live with, and so will we (that may be the greatest miracle yet)! Here I am reminded of the old adage, "To live above with the saints we love, o how that will be glory. To live below with the saints we know, now that's a different story!"

"How will we feel if people we love are not there?

SYDNEY, AGE 9

Given the fact that there will be great multitudes of people not in Zion—all those who have not called on the name of Jesus, not exercised saving faith in him, and not lived to the glory of God—how will we be able to deal with this? We have addressed this issue briefly but it might pay to say the same thing again but in a different way. How can we be happy knowing some people, possibly loved ones, are in Hell? This question has been discussed for at least several hundred years (before that Christians apparently saw no problem to be resolved). Several answers have been put forward that attempt to show that eternal happiness is not at odds with an eternal Hell. Some argue that in the resurrection we shall have no knowledge of those who are in Hell. Others argue that we shall be so overcome with bliss that nothing could disturb this happiness. Neither of these views seems convincing to me. To not know of parents or children, close friends or spouses, if they are non-believers seems incompatible with the fact that our personal identities will continue for eternity. The idea that our bliss will be such that nothing can dent our happiness is a good general principle; I can go along with that, but it lacks something.

The final view that has been offered, and the one I tend to agree with, is that in the presence of God we will see the nature of evil with sufficient clarity that we will be at peace with the reality that some of our loved ones have unfortunately chosen Hell over Heaven. Here the argument is that the more like God we become, the more like Christ we think, feel, and act. God can look on the just and the unjust, the saved and the unsaved, and not be overcome with sadness. More concretely, the incarnate Son, Jesus Christ, could look upon his fellow Jews who were turning away from him,

6. Helm, *Last Things*, 92.

and so away from God, and lament that fact, feel saddened by this reality, but not be overcome by this sadness (Matt 23:35–39). I firmly believe that in the resurrection we too will have new ways of seeing, through the eyes of the Holy Spirit, and will be able to affirm the goodness and love of God's just judgment amidst the saddening loss of loved ones. This will take a miracle on God's part, of course, but that is what the resurrection is: a grand miracle. It is hard to even contemplate this possibility now, but in God's goodness he will overcome all impossibilities.

I admit this topic is a difficult one for us to think about and it is even more difficult to come to clear conclusions about such things. However, an educated attempt to answer these types of questions is required of us and I hope what I have shared above is enough to move you to contemplate how you might answer the same questions. These are serious matters and we want to be sure we give answers that, to the best of our ability, are pleasing to the Lord. I hope I have said enough to orient you toward an answer but have not too much to put you off thinking through these issues for yourself. Moving on now from the sublime to the ridiculous, or perhaps more accurately, from issues of life and death to issues of a less crucial nature, I want to pick up on the status of animals, especially pets, and ask about their presence in Zion.

How we might answer the question of what animals might be like in Zion and whether any of our pets might make it there? I have already affirmed the presence of animals in Zion. Whether it is a glimpse into the so-called millennial kingdom (a period of time some believe will preempt the end of this world and the new heavens and earth) or not, Isaiah 11:1–9 does paint a clear picture of what life will be like when God reorders creation. There we read of wolves and bears, leopards and snakes, lions and lambs, sheep and cattle, and many other animals, all living in harmony and peace (Isa 65:17, 25). This is the easy part of the issue. What animals will be like, how they will act, what they will eat, and how they will flourish in relation to humanity is harder to answer. A more speculative but important issue for children (and many adults) is the question of whether or not pets might be in Zion. We will deal with the question of pets in the next section after we examine more concretely some of the issues raised by having animal companions in the renewed creation.

A biblical theology of animals would show that God created animals for humans. We are tasked with their care (Gen 1:28) and it is a delight for us to turn all of nature, animals especially, back to the Creator so that he is praised through their flourishing (Ps 8:6–8). Part of being a faithful follower of God is the care of animals (Prov 12:10). David, a man after God's own heart, had a special love of animals (2 Sam 12:3). In Zion, it is to be expected that we too will have a love for all animals, and have the compulsion to care for them and see them prosper. As Randy Alcorn provocatively stated, "Adam, Noah, and Jesus are the three heads of the three Earths. When Adam was created, God surrounded him with animals. When Noah was delivered from the Flood, God surrounded him with animals. When Jesus was born, God surrounded him with animals. When Jesus establishes the renewed Earth, with renewed men and women, don't you think he'll surround himself with renewed animals?"[7]

The question of what animals will eat is hard to answer. If, as is the case with humans, food is not required for survival, it is possible that animals will not need to eat but may choose to do so for pure enjoyment. If this is the case then carnivores, like the big cats, for instance, would cease being dangerous to humans in Zion for they simply will not have an instinctual desire to eat flesh (Isaiah 11, 65). The lust for blood and flesh would be gone and in its place instincts of play, of adventure, and of a safe but untamed freedom would remain. C. S. Lewis dreamt of lions, saying that "when he has ceased to be dangerous, will still be awful: indeed, that we shall then first see that of which the present fangs and claws are a clumsy, and satanically perverted, imitation. There will still be something like the shaking of a golden mane: and often the good Duke will say, 'Let him roar again.'"[8]

> "Does Jesus have a pet?"
>
> EMMA, AGED 5

Perhaps this is how humans and wildlife will coexist. More speculatively again, and let's not dwell too long on this one. Perhaps there will be different sorts of animal life, lower and higher. The higher forms of animal life may very well be changed in the ways indicated above while the lower forms of animal life may be, bluntly put, food for other animals and for humans. We may barbeque in Zion yet. Whatever the case, we know there will be no death, no pain, and nothing to fear.

Such are the biblical and theological components of who will and won't be in Zion. What remains is a brief discussion of how we might play with these concepts a little more.

7. Alcorn, *Heaven*, 395.

8. Lewis, *Problem of Pain*, 147.

Let's Play

Trying to conceive of what the new heavens and earth will be like is scintillating. I hope you have felt something of this as you have read this book. God does not answer all our questions in Scripture, but he has drawn the curtain back at a few points and allowed us to peek behind it and develop an idea of what is to come. In this final section, we have to play with a few of the ideas we have introduced, especially when it comes to animals on the new earth.

When it comes to humanity the picture is clear enough: followers of Christ on earth can be assured of an eternal life in the resurrection with Christ in Zion. The burden on each of us is to see that we communicate the gospel as clearly as possible and that we embody it as faithfully as we can. God must and will do the rest. Zion will be a society of saints, a fellowship of believers, a world of women and men who are passionately in love with the triune God and with each other and all of creation. Zion will be a worshipping community representing a vast array of languages, cultures, and customs. But—and this is a big but (yes, the children can giggle at that)—Zion is a unity of unlikes, a world of unity not despite but on the basis of our differences. C. S. Lewis once wrote:

> Heaven is a city, and a Body, because the blessed remain eternally different: a society, because each has something to tell all the others—fresh and ever fresh news of the 'My God' whom each finds in Him whom all praise as 'Our God.' For doubtless the continually successful, yet never complete, attempt by each soul to communicate its unique vision to all others (and that by means whereof earthly art and philosophy are but clumsy imitations) is also among the ends for which the individual was created.[9]

"Will our family dog go to Heaven?"

EDEN, AGE 7

When it comes to animals, and especially our pets, the situation is very different. Billy Graham is said to have made the statement, "God will prepare everything for our perfect happiness in heaven, and if it takes my dog being there, I believe he'll be there."[10]

9. Ibid., 155.

10. Graham, in the *Philadelphia Inquirer*, February 7, 1999, cited in *Ask Billy Graham*, 216.

More humorously, Will Rogers one said, "If there are no dogs in Heaven, then when I die I want to go where they went."[11] I'm not sure what sort of dogs Billy Graham or Will Rogers had, but they must have been good companions. While Graham's and Rogers's comments have sentimental value, they are not really a strong enough argument to think our pets will be resurrected. We have to look elsewhere for this argument. It is more than a little interesting that some of the most respected evangelical thinkers today believe that some pets will be resurrected—only good pets, not the bad ones, and possibly only pets of believers: people such as C. S. Lewis, Rick Warren, John Piper, and Billy Graham, not to mention some significant names from the past such as St. John of the Cross, St. Francis of Assisi, Martin Luther, and John Wesley.

The Scriptures—from first to last—suggest that animals have souls (the Hebrew word is *nephesh*). Both Moses in Genesis and John in Revelation communicate that the Creator endowed animals with souls (see Gen 1:30; 2:7; 6:17; 7:15, 22; Rev 8:9). Throughout the history of the church, the classic understanding of living things has included the doctrine that animals as well as humans have souls. These are different than the souls of humans, to be sure, but they are ensouled creatures none the less. We also know that with Christ's death the animal kingdom was an indirect but intentional beneficiary. Romans 8:21–23 reads:

> The creation itself will be liberated from its bondage to decay and brought into the freedom and glory of the children of God. We know that the whole creation has been groaning as in the pains of childbirth right up to the present time. Not only so, but we ourselves, who have the firstfruits of the Spirit, groan inwardly as we wait eagerly for our adoption to sonship, the redemption of our bodies.

Christ did not die for the sins of animals or for their personal salvation. Animals are not sinners and Christ did not redeem them as he did humanity. But Christ's death is clearly of benefit to all of creation, animals included. C. S. Lewis once proposed:

> The theory I am suggesting . . . makes God the centre of the universe and man the subordinate centre of terrestrial nature: the beasts are not co-ordinate with man, but subordinate to him, and their destiny is through and through related to his. And the derivative immortality suggested for them is not a mere amende or

11. Rogers, *Connecticut Yankee*.

compensation: It is part and parcel of the new heaven and new
earth, organically related to the whole suffering process of the
world's fall and redemption.[12]

In the Old Testament we repeatedly read of God's delight in his creatures and it even hints at a future destiny for them when in Psalm 104 we
read:

> How many are your works, Lord!
> In wisdom you made them all;
> the earth is full of your creatures.
> There is the sea, vast and spacious,
> teeming with creatures beyond number—
> living things both large and small.
> There the ships go to and fro,
> and Leviathan, which you formed to frolic there.
> All creatures look to you
> to give them their food at the proper time.
> When you give it to them,
> they gather it up;
> when you open your hand,
> they are satisfied with good things.
> When you hide your face,
> they are terrified;
> when you take away their breath,
> they die and return to the dust.
> When you send your Spirit,
> they are created,
> and you renew the face of the ground.

A number of biblical commentators see in this last verse (v. 30) a reference to the fact that God will recreate certain animals after they have died
in order to renew the face of the earth. We can't be certain about this, but it
is a clear possibility.

If the argument above holds any weight, then I think it opens the door
to believe that extinct animals will be our companions in Zion. Imagine
shepherding some of the great dinosaurs like a Gorgon (a smaller, faster
T-Rex), or marveling at the Moa (a twelve-foot-tall flightless bird endemic

12. Lewis, *Problem of Pain*, 145.

to New Zealand), giggling at the sight of a Quagga (half zebra, half horse), and actually seeing an Irish elk (seven feet tall with twelve-foot antlers)!

But again, what of our pets? I think the only argument robust enough to be plausible is one based on the fact that one of the things God created humanity to do was to care for and steward the welfare of animals. Some of these animals become dear to us, friends and companions (pets), and as such they become related to us and precious. Loving an animal is not like loving a human, and it is certainly not like loving an inanimate object (a "Pet Rock," for instance, made popular in 1975 by Gary Dahl[13]). Some people can't dream of a life without their phone or computer, but that is different. There is a relational connection between some people

> "Will I be brave enough to put my head underwater in Heaven?"
>
> MICAH, AGE 5

and their animals and it is not out of the question that such animals (pets) will be recreated on the new earth. Echoing this thought, John Piper published a poem on the end times that included this stanza:

> And as I knelt beside the brook
> To drink eternal life, I took
> A glance across the golden grass,
> And saw my dog, old Blackie, fast
> As she could come. She leaped the stream
> Almost—and what a happy gleam
> Was in her eye. I knelt to drink,
> And knew that I was on the brink
> Of endless joy. And everywhere
> I turned I saw a wonder there.
> That's old John Younge with both legs on.
> The blind can see a bird on wing,
> The dumb can lift their voice and sing.
> The diabetic eats at will,
> The coronary runs uphill.[14]

13. On the Pet Rock fad see Tamara Weston, "Pet Rocks."

14. Piper, *Purifying Power*, 381. Piper appears to have changed his mind by 2015, thinking the idea of pets in Heaven is pure sentimentality, good enough for a four-year-old but not for an adult. See http://www.desiringgod.org/interviews/do-pets-go-to-heaven.

Notice what I am *not* saying. I am not suggesting animals are immortal, nor am I suggesting they can be saved. What I am suggesting—and it is only that—is that if there is a sufficient relational bond between a human and an animal then perhaps that animal may yet make an appearance on the new earth *for the sake of the human.* Here C. S. Lewis's wisdom and imagination are again useful. He writes, ". . . it seems to me possible that certain animals may have an immortality, not in themselves, but in the immortality of their masters. And the difficulty about personal identity in a creature barely personal disappears when the creature is thus kept in its proper context."[15]

On this basis, I think we would be right to talk with our children about the possibility of pets going to the new heaven and earth. However, it would also be useful to remind them that even if pets are not present what God has in store for us will be more than we could ever imagine or hope for and we will not be sad or lonely. Not that this will be heard by them first time round. When I discussed this with my children all they could think about was how good God is in letting our little black cat, Christmas Star (Star for short), into Zion to be with us forever. I, however, was not so excited by this prospect.

Children often have worries over eternal life. They can think they will be lonely, won't know anyone, or might not be accepted there. What we learn from God is just the opposite. We will never be lonely, we will all be family there, and possibly even some of our pets will be with us too.

Summary

In this chapter I have tried to communicate the following:

- God the Father, Son, and Holy Spirit, the host of angels, and those savingly united to Christ will be in Zion.

- A great multitude of animals will also populate the new earth.

- Fallen angels (Satan and his demons) and those who have not chosen to faithfully follow Christ will not be found in Zion.

- God will miraculously arrange for us to handle the fact that some of our loved ones may not be in Zion.

15. Lewis, *Problem of Pain*, 144.

- It is possible that some pets and animals of great significance to some humans will be recreated and may yet walk the new earth.

- Zion will be full of a great multitude of believers from every age and every culture.

Chapter 6

Conclusion: On Eating Pie in the Sky

We are very shy nowadays of even mentioning heaven. We are
afraid of the jeer about "pie in the sky," and of being told that we
are trying to "escape" from the duty of making a happy world
here and now into dreams of a happy world elsewhere. But
either there is "pie in the sky" or there is not. If there is not, then
Christianity is false, for this doctrine is woven into its whole
fabric.[1]

C. S. LEWIS

Jesus came to bring not simply moral precepts but the reality of
a new world order that revolutionizes the whole of life.[2]

DONALD G. BLOESCH

Narnia and Middle Earth make for great stories, and so does a new heaven
and earth; the difference between them is that Heaven is true. I don't claim
to be an expert in children's ministry, nor am I an expert in human development, psychology, or sociology. But I am a dad with a theological doctorate,
who feels the burden to correct my children's taunts that I am a doctor—
"but not the useful kind." I live out of the conviction, proven true so often
in my own life, that theology is practical, and the doctrine academics call

1. Lewis, *Problem of Pain*, 149.
2. Bloesch, *Last Things*, 19.

"eschatology" and everyone else calls "all that crazy end-times stuff" is as practical as it comes. Understanding what God has told us about the afterlife is as important as it is useful. Christians throughout church history have gained a profound hope in God's teaching on the future and this has practically shaped the way they lived. Reflecting on the end times actually invigorates our work and play in the present. It gives us an orientation to our lives, it helps us understand how to live in between the times, and it provides us with a way to keep Christ central amidst the often chaotic activity of our daily lives. Children, perhaps more than the rest of us, need this kind of stability, this kind of framework, and these kinds of foundations to build their lives upon.

In this final chapter, I want to address one final set of questions that lurk about whenever the end times are discussed. The first question concerns the issue of how practical this doctrine is: Does this make us too heavenly minded to be of any earthly good? I clearly don't agree with that sentiment, as I believe God teaches us about what is to come for very specific reasons, namely, to fill us with hope, to offer us assurance about life after life after death, and to teach us how to die well. A second question relates to the here-and-now in relation to the future: To what extent does Heaven begin on earth? Each of these deserves some discussion before we conclude. We will tackle the second question first.

Heaven on Earth?

To know that God has more in store for us than we could ever possibly imagine is a wonderful thing (Eph 3:20). To experience this in part now is Heaven on earth. Heaven begins on earth in one way, but in another way it begins only at death. In Ephesians we read that saints are already, in one sense, in the heavenlies with Christ (Eph 2:6). Heaven begins on earth by union with Christ. The believer experiences a *foretaste* of Heaven now. They already possess Heaven in the sense that they now experience something of the quality of the life to come. Foretaste equals: "Although no eye has seen. No ear has heard, nor mind conceived the things that God has in store for his church, he reveals them to his children" (1 Cor 2:9). Not in the form of a secret code for the initiated, but as Paul reminds us, "by the Spirit." This seems to imply that we are talking about spiritual realities at this point. Hence the Christian experiences Heaven now, in part, through being a child of God.

In a real sense, the spiritual runs ahead of the physical when it comes to Heaven. The body remains liable to corruption while the human spirit rejoices in the hope of the glory of God. At the resurrection, that imbalance will be redressed. "Then this mortal must put on immortality, and this corruptible must put on incorruption" (1 Cor 15:53).

So while Heaven has already begun for the believer there is an equally clear sense in which Heaven is yet to be. Hebrews 11:10 describes it as a city that God *has* built. Jesus said it was a home he *is* preparing (John 14:3). And Peter writes of the inheritance, incorruptible and undefiled and unfading, that is *reserved* in Heaven for the Christian (1 Pet 1:4).

This leads me to the conviction that God wants us to bring a Christian imagination to bear upon the issues of the life to come in order to inspire, inflame, and enlarge our vision of what is to come. When this type of Christian imagination kicks in, Heaven ceases to be pie-in-the-sky-till-I-die theology and becomes a life-giving stream of truth spurring us on to good works. We know it to be true given that whenever the church has faced persecution one of the key doctrines to come out of the woodwork and comfort God's people has been eschatology. When God's people Israel were in exile in Babylon they sang songs of their promised return home (Psalm 137). When some of God's people in America were being enslaved they sang songs of hope and redemption, songs like "Swing Low, Sweet Chariot."[3] A Christian imagination about the new heavens and the new earth has always been a practical dreaming—and may it ever be so.

When it comes to end-times theology, one of three positions is normally adopted.[4] One can adopt a *despairing resignation* in which we give up on any hopes for the future and no longer participate meaningfully in the world in order to look for and work toward solutions to worldly problems. But "we cannot afford the luxury of despair," writes Hans Schwartz, before reminding us that "many do drop out of the future-directed stream of life and dull their minds with drugs, alcohol, and medications of all sorts."[5] When this ideology takes hold within Christian circles the future into which God is calling the church and moving the world is underplayed, ignored, or simply not believed in. When this happens a profound loss of

3. "Swing Low, Sweet Chariot" is thought to have been written by Wallis Willis, a Choctaw freedman who lived near the county seat of Hugo, Oklahoma, sometime before 1862. The Fisk Jubilee Singers of Fisk University recorded the song in 1909. The song enjoyed a resurgence during the 1960s civil rights struggle.

4. The following three positions are adapted from Schwartz, *Eschatology*, 405–7.

5. Ibid., 405.

hope ensues and with it a resignation to the ways of the world. Churches look little different from the culture that surrounds them and as such they lose almost any sense of mission as they cease to live as radically counter-cultural signposts to the kingdom of God.

Without wanting to sound too dire, I do think that many Western churches are too myopic (short-sighted) for their own good. Many churches have tended to pull back on preaching and teaching on the afterlife and, as a result, other things have rushed in to fill the vacuum created by the absence of a firm hope for the new heavens and earth. Schwartz mentions drugs, alcohol, and medications, and I think we could add to that list an unbalanced quest for immediate experience, a lust for entertainment, and a disproportionate passion for what many call "relevance." In our desire to be relevant to society we often look like we have converted from Christianity to our culture. If we look the same, talk the same, think the same, and live the same, one would be hard-pressed to say we are not the same. This position underappreciates God's teaching about what is to come.

A second position often adopted in regards to the end times is that of some form of *futurist activism*. *Futurist* because the future so dominates one's life that the present is seen as merely a minor inconvenience (people included) as we work towards our real life. In the meantime, many seek to bring Heaven to earth in its fullness now (*activism*), without waiting for Christ! This manifested itself a generation or two ago when various societies flouted with the idea of Marxist socialism, the attempt to bring in a classless utopia. While Marxism is for all intents and purposes dead, what has filled this vacuum is the New Age and neo-pagan movements. "While both its protest and its vision are well taken, we should note that it shares with all other messianic movements the lack of the true Messiah."[6]

Speaking from within the context of a professed Christianity, many have transplanted their future-directed vision of life to come into the present and have adopted a health-and-wealth gospel or a signs-and-wonders fetish. That is to say, some Christians overestimate the present time and confuse it with the future, seeking to make this fallen world God's final kingdom now. They literally want to make Heaven on earth *now*. The problem is, it isn't. Sin, death, and disease will be eliminated, in part now but only fully in the future. To confuse what time the church is in is deadly to people's faith.

6. Ibid., 406–7.

The final position adopted in regards to God's teaching about what is to come could be summarized by the term *active anticipation*. This is a position unique to Christianity. Knowing that the future has already begun in the resurrection of Jesus Christ, it dares to anticipate this future amidst the travail of this world. Those adopting this Christian position are not naïve enough to think that this world can be redeemed by human effort alone, nor are they pessimistic and assume that the world is "going to hell in a hand basket" (proverbially speaking). Rather:

> this process of active anticipation strives for a better humanity, a more just society, and a more worldly world to live in. But since it is only anticipation, Christian faith is realistic enough to take into account our intrinsic alienation from God, who is the source of all wisdom and all good things. Thus we must reject the illusion that we could ever create a good humanity, a just society, or a new world. Ultimate perfection and removal of death as the dimensional border between our world and the new world to come will be brought about by God's gracious action, undeserved by us.[7]

We currently live in between the times. Christ is risen and rules from his throne in Heaven. We wait with eager and active anticipation for his second coming, to make all things new. We live now in light of eternity.

Living in Light of Eternity

There are many ways in which thinking about what is to come prepares us for what we currently experience. In this final section, I simply want to point to two things that thinking, talking, praying, and living in light of eternity brings us: hope and assurance, both of which enable us to live well.

Earlier we had the opportunity to define hope and discuss it in a little detail. Here I want to remind you of the benefits a confident expectation that what is currently unseen will one day come true (a biblical definition of hope) brings. Elihu was wrong about Job but right about God when he said it is God "who gives songs in the night" (Job 35:10). When bad things happen to us—when relationships break up, when cancer sneaks in and threatens to steal a loved one away, or when life throws us a curve ball and things get screwed up—we need to know that God loves us and is for us and has a plan for us.

7. Ibid., 407.

The Reformer Martin Luther is said to have penned a short poem that is worth repeating here in English (whether he did write this or not is disputed, but it is a good poem).

Feelings come and feelings go,
And feelings are deceiving;
My warrant is the Word of God—
Naught else is worth believing.

Though all my heart should feel condemned
For want of some sweet token,
There is One greater than my heart
Whose Word cannot be broken.[8]

Luther knew that our feelings are fickle and often deceive us. When it *feels* like our prayers bounce off the ceiling and God has abandoned us, we need to remind ourselves of what we know to be true. God has told us a lot about eternity, about our future resurrection, and about the beautiful and eventful new heavens and earth he is preparing for us, where there is no pain, sorrow, or sickness. We need to trust in God and hope in his promises of future grace. I know of no more effective way to do this than thinking about what the triune God of grace and glory has done for us, is doing for us, and *will* yet do for us. David Calhoun reminds us that:

The psalmist prayed, "Uphold me according to your promise, that I may live, and let me not be put to shame in my hope" (Ps. 119:116). The apostle rejoiced "in the hope of the glory of God," confident this hope does "not put us to shame" (Rom. 5:2, 5). Paul told the Christians in Colossae that their hope was laid up for them "in heaven" (Col 1:15). These two words, *hope* and *heaven*, belong together. We now "hope for what we do not see," but in that day we will see and hope will become heaven (Rom. 8:25).[9]

How different Christian hope is from the hopelessness of the world! Contemporary culture often throws up examples of when people wrestle

---

8. There is no reliable reference to this poem coming from Luther, but it is routinely attributed to him. Its actual origins are unknown but it is completely consistent with the tenor of Luther's theology and life. If you are a child of the 80s and 90s like I am, you might appreciate listening to Greg X Volz of Petra fame singing this ditty here: https://www.youtube.com/watch?v=zIPxSL6Uzlg.

9. Calhoun, "Hope of Heaven," 248.

with the idea of hope and hopelessness. I am reminded of the haunting song by Chris Rea, "Tell Me There's a Heaven," one of the most honest secular songs I have heard, where he sings:

> The little girl, she said to me
> "What are these things that I can see?
> Each night when I come home from school
> When Mama calls me in for tea"
> Oh, every night a baby dies
> And every night a mama cries
> What makes those men do what they do?
> To make that person black and blue
> Grandpa says they're happy now
> They sit with God in paradise
> With Angels' wings and still somehow
> It makes me feel like ice
>
> Tell me there's a Heaven
> Tell me that it's true
> Tell me there's a reason
> Why I'm seeing what I do
> Tell me there's a Heaven
> Where all those people go
> Tell me they're all happy now
> Papa, tell me that it's so
>
> So, do I tell her that it's true?
> That there's a place for me and you
> Where hungry children smile and say
> We wouldn't have no other way
> That every painful crack of bones
> Is a step along the way
> Every wrong done is a game plan
> To that great and joyful day
>
> And I'm looking
> At the father and the son
> And I'm looking

At the mother and the daughter
And I'm watching them in tears of pain
And I'm watching them suffer
Don't tell that little girl
Tell me

Tell me there's a Heaven
Tell me that it's true
Tell me there's a reason
Why I'm seeing what I do

Tell me there's a Heaven
Where all those people go
Tell me they're all happy now
Papa, tell me that it's so.[10]

What a moving and very telling song. It expresses hope without foundation, faith without content, grief without resolution, and life without purpose. And we could amplify this hopelessness with many other examples.

In 1997 the rock band (the best rock band in the world!) Bon Jovi released an album that contained a rarely heard song entitled "August 7, 4:15."[11] The song was written in memory of Katherine Korzilius, daughter of Jon Bon Jovi's former personal manager. On August 7, 1996, six-year-old Katherine was dropped off at her mailbox approximately an eighth of a mile from their house so that she could walk home. An hour later Katherine had not returned home. Katherine's body was eventually found dead in the middle of the road one mile from her house, killed due to a suspected hit-and-run. Her murderer is yet to be found. In the opening words of the song we hear the anguished cry, "I think God closed his eyes and the world got mean." Throughout the song the constant refrain is, "Tell me it was just a dream—August 7, 4:15, God closed his eyes and the world got mean—August 7, 4:15." The words echo the heartfelt pain of Katherine's parents and friends who are struggling to find answers to why this could happen. Who do they blame? Where do they turn? What can they do?

10. Chris Rea, "Tell Me There's a Heaven," *Road to Hell* (Warner Bros., 1989).

11. Bon Jovi, "August 7, 4:15," *Destination Anywhere* (Mercury, 1997). The official music video for the song looks to be no longer available online. It starred A-list actors like Demi Moore and developed a story independent of the facts of the Korzilius case. You can watch a related video here: https://www.youtube.com/watch?v=D9fxB-6SWsk.

In the official music video that accompanied the song, the wife clams up, suffering depression and guilt. The husband seeks to help his wife but can't get through to her. The song is gloomy, depressing, and offers no hope. In the music video, the wife is seen reciting a poem: "Condemned the world to a perpetual winter." She eventually blames her husband for the death of their daughter. *He* should have protected her. *He* should have been there.

In part two of the official music video, the husband finds his wife's scrapbook. He opens it to find it filled with pictures of their lost baby, and repeatedly scribbled, "Why, why, why?" The scrapbook is a gallery of guilt, unresolved pain, and blame. He writes in the scrapbook, "What's it gonna take to make you believe in me?" Eventually, the wife steals a baby from the hospital she works in, the husband finds her, and they both fall to the ground crying. "O God," he exclaims in vain, as the video ends, "Tell me it was just a dream—August 7, 4:15, God closed his eyes and the world got mean—August 7, 4:15." The song and the video are miserably hopeless.

Where can people turn in the face of tragedy, suffering, and loss? Who can people turn to for answers? Does God close his eyes on our suffering and pain? Can he really just turn the other way? In light of what we now know about eternity, I think it is safe to say people can turn to Christians for answers and we can point them to Christ for hope and assurance. Hope and assurance go hand in hand. Assurance is that conviction we have that God is good . . . and he is good for us, despite what current events and our emotions might tell us. We have an assured hope, and we have this not because of some pie-in-the-sky idea, and not because of wishful thinking. Rather, we have an assurance of faith based upon the risen Jesus Christ.

Eschatology (what we believe about the things to come) is not simply about conjecturing about the future; it has more to do with what *Christ* is doing and will do. Likewise, the book of Revelation is not simply about disclosing what is going to happen as much as it is about further revealing who *Jesus* is and what *he* is doing. It is a revelation of Jesus more than an unveiling of what is to come. In short, the Bible's teaching focuses on the *Eschatos* (Greek for the "Last One," Jesus Christ), not the *eschata* (Greek for the "last things"). German theologian Hans Schwartz helpfully reminds us that:

> Union with God, abolition of anguish and sorrow, and permanent
> beauty and perfection seem so unreal to our life of alienation, pain
> and suffering, transition and change that we are about to discard
> these hopes as utopian dreams. We would be right in so doing if

Jesus Christ had not shown us through his death and resurrection that this fulfillment is attainable. Because of Jesus Christ and the promise contained for us in the Christ event, the hope for a final realization of such a destiny is a realistic hope.[12]

In 1 Thessalonians 4:13–14 Paul teaches us, under divine inspiration, "Brothers and sisters, we do not want you to be uninformed about those who sleep in death, so that you do not grieve like the rest of mankind, who have no hope. For we believe that Jesus died and rose again, and so we believe that God will bring with Jesus those who have fallen asleep in him." How does this look different in real life? I am reminded of a story I read years ago now in *Christianity Today* magazine entitled "Two Minutes to Eternity." It was written by Marshall Shelley and briefly told of the death of *two* of his children.[13] When I first read the story I cried. When I read it now I cry. And when I preach on this topic and use this story I cry. I'm crying now.

Marshall Shelley's son died of a chromosome abnormality. "As far as I was concerned, this was a design flaw. The designer was directly responsible," he writes. The doctor advised Marshall and his wife Susan to abort the baby when the problem was initially diagnosed. In an amazing testimony of faith, Susan responded, "We believe God is the giver and taker of life. If the only opportunity I have to know this child is in my womb, I don't want to cut that time short. If the only world he is to know is the womb, I want that world to be as safe as I can make it." They left the medical center stunned. Susan said to her husband, "Pregnancy is hard enough when you know you're going to leave the hospital with a baby. I don't know how I can go through the pain of childbirth knowing I won't have a child to hold."

The parents had prayed to God that if it was at all possible would he allow the baby to at least experience the breath of life. That prayer was answered. The baby was born and they saw its chest rise . . . and fall—the breath of life. But then he turned blue and passed away.

"Do you have a name for the baby?" Asked the nurse.

"Toby," Susan replied, "A biblical name short for Tobiah—God is faithful."

Three months later an elder daughter, Mandy, also died, just short of her second birthday. She was severely mentally disabled.

---

12. Schwartz, *Eschatology*, 403.

13. Shelley, "Two Minutes to Eternity."

In the face of severe loss and grief, where could the Shelleys turn? Was there a way out of the impasse depression had created? Could they get through this? What happened next is truly amazing. Mr. Shelley writes:

> Not long after we buried Toby and Mandy, our seven-year-old daughter, Stacey, told us she heard God's voice in the middle of the night telling her that "Mandy and Toby are very busy. They are building our house, and they are guarding his throne." Not knowing how to respond to a child who had never offered a claim like that before, I found myself reading the Bible with renewed interest in descriptions of heavenly activities. Was this message consistent with Scripture? Our family discussions usually focused on heaven.

In desperation, agony, and helplessness, Marshall and Susan turned to Scripture for guidance. Where else could they turn? And their attention was drawn to the new heavens and earth. They saw that Heaven is a place of intense activity, of work, and of worship. They saw that Zion is our home that Jesus is preparing for those that love him. Marshall wrote, "What is clear is that heaven will be a place of active duty. Even after the ultimate spiritual battle is over, our responsibilities continue."

Marshall Shelley concluded his story with these moving words:

> I can't be specific about how we will assist in reigning with Christ. But those tasks sound like they have more significance than most careers we pursue in our lifetimes. Could it be that when I finally start the most significant service of my life, I will find that this is that for which I was truly created for? I may find I was created not for what I would accomplish on earth, but for the role I will fulfil in heaven. Why did God create a child to live two minutes? He didn't. God created Toby for eternity. He created each of us for eternity, where we may be surprised to find our true calling, which always seemed just out of reach here on earth.

How different this response is to the anguished cries of Eric Clapton over the loss of his son, or Chris Rea's hopeless questioning over the deaths inflicted through wars, or Bon Jovi's lament for a child's hit-and-run. Christians who know whose they are and what they are destined for will find hope and assurance to live this life for all its worth. The Shelleys didn't just survive the death of their two children; they were enabled to thrive, as they await the great resurrection and life everlasting in the city of God—with Toby and Mandy by their side. As renowned German theologian Wolfhart Pannenberg once wrote, "Only one who is certain of the future can relax and turn to today's business."[14] I have my own personal stories of such hope and assurance at work in my life, and I know other dear friends with similar testimonies, like that of my friends (and my boss) Charles and Joanne Hewlett, who style this a *hurting hope*.[15] The reality of the risen Christ brings us hope and assurance that the best is yet to come.

And That Is All I Have to Say about That

The gallant mouse Reepicheep, in C. S. Lewis's *The Voyage of the Dawn Treader*, is the quintessential figure in children's literature of one who knows he was created for another world and will stop at nothing to get there, spreading the good news of Aslan (Jesus) along the way. Like a modern-day parable of the pearl of great price (Matt 13:45–46), Reepicheep is adamant:

> My own plans are made. While I can, I sail east in the Dawn Treader. When she fails me, I paddle east in my coracle. When she sinks, I shall swim east with my four paws. And when I can swim no longer, if I have not reached Aslan's country, or shot over the edge of the world, in some vast cataract, I shall sink with my nose to the sunrise.[16]

In Reepicheep Lewis gives us a glimpse of how life might be lived when the new heavens and earth are in view. Lewis knows what all saints throughout history knew: it is those who care most for the next world who do the most for this.

When we know what the triune God has in store for us in the new heavens and earth, all fear is dispelled, all sorrow is muted, and hope rises within us like a burning coal. As a result, we live different lives now. Our lives become evidence that our treasure is in Heaven and not in this world. The fleeting pleasures of this world begin to lose their attraction and so their hold over us. We rely on the God who will raise us from the dead (2 Cor 1:9), and revel in the hope of the glory of God (Rom 5:2). As a direct result, we are less likely to give in to the evil desires of our heart here and now. "Instead," writes John Piper, "we savor the wonder that the Owner and Ruler of the universe loves us, and has destined us for the enjoyment of his glory, and is working infallibly to bring us to his eternal kingdom. So we

14. Pannenberg, *What Is Man?*, 44.
15. Hewlett and Hewlett, *Hurting Hope*.
16. Lewis, *Voyage of the Dawn Treader*, 21.

live to meet the needs of others, because God is living to meet our needs (Isaiah 64:4; 41:10; 2 Chronicles 16:9; Psalm 23:6). We love our enemies, and do good, and bless those who curse us and pray for those who despise us, because we are not enslaved to the fleeting, petty pleasures that come from returning evil for evil, and we know that our reward is great in heaven (Luke 6:35; Matthew 5:45; 1 Peter 3:9)."[17]

That brings us to the end of our time together. I do hope you have heard God's voice speak to you through Scripture, and I pray you have had your mind and your soul enlarged through thinking about what God has in store for those who love him. Now, in the fashion of the saints before us, go and gossip the good news to all and sundry—to spouse and children, to brother and sister, to saints and sinners alike. The last word, however, goes to God:

> Then I saw "a new heaven and a new earth," for the first heaven and the first earth had passed away, and there was no longer any sea. I saw the Holy City, the new Jerusalem, coming down out of heaven from God, prepared as a bride beautifully dressed for her husband. And I heard a loud voice from the throne saying, "Look! God's dwelling place is now among the people, and he will dwell with them. They will be his people, and God himself will be with them and be their God. 'He will wipe every tear from their eyes. There will be no more death' or mourning or crying or pain, for the old order of things has passed away."
>
> He who was seated on the throne said, "I am making everything new!" Then he said, "Write this down, for these words are trustworthy and true."
>
> He said to me: "It is done. I am the Alpha and the Omega, the Beginning and the End. To the thirsty I will give water without cost from the spring of the water of life. Those who are victorious will inherit all this, and I will be their God and they will be my children. (Rev 21:1–7)

Summary

In this chapter I have tried to communicate the following:

- Understanding what God has told us about the afterlife is as important as it is useful.

17. Piper, *Purifying Power*, 369–70.

- A Christian imagination about the new heavens and the new earth has always been a practical way of dreaming.

- Heaven begins on earth by union with Christ.

- Knowing what is to come develops within us a hopeful anticipation.

- Hope and assurance flow directly from thinking about the end times.

- Faith in Christ and what he is doing and what he is going to do enables us to live life to the fullest now.

Study Guides

Chapter 1: Introduction: An Inkling of What's to Come

Family Study Guide

1. Ask your children what they think Heaven will be like.

2. What are they most looking forward to? What concerns do they have?

3. Do you find it unusual to think of your job as a parent as like that of a priest? Myk gives several examples of how he acts as a priest to his children. Talk with your family about how you do that too.

4. How important to do you think it is to have a "Christian imagination"?

5. Read the book or watch the movie *Heaven Is for Real* and have a discussion after it about how the children feel about what they saw and heard.

6. Make a list of questions your family has about Heaven and then revisit these throughout your reading of the book. (Any unanswered questions could be directed to Myk by email or you could consult some of the resources listed at the end of the book.)

7. There is an "Easter egg" hidden in this book. Can you find it? (Hint: 6 chapters + 6 letters = . . .)

Adults Study Guide

1. Do you believe there is a Heaven?

2. What do you think Heaven will be like?

3. Why do you believe what you believe about Heaven? That is, how can we know if what we believe about the afterlife is true?

4. What are you most looking forward to? What concerns do you have?

5. Apart from parenting, where else might we act as priests to others?

6. How important to do you think it is to have a "Christian (baptized) imagination"?

7. There is an "Easter egg" hidden in this book. Can you find it?

Chapter 2: The Best of All Possible Worlds
(What Is Heaven Like?)

Family Study Guide

1. Using the word *heaven* to speak of three places—the sky, God's current home, and our final destination—is confusing. See if your family can settle on three different names for these three different places (e.g., sky, heaven, new earth; or sky, Paradise, new heavens and earth; or . . . ?).

2. Myk made the statement that "Heaven is not in our space-time continuum." By this he meant you can't find God's current abode in a spaceship and the new heavens and earth will not simply be a continuation of space and time as we now know it. What children's movies or books might help our families grasp this idea a little? (The TARDIS could help, or the wardrobe in *The Chronicles of Narnia*, or some of the music from Christian children's band Butterflyfish . . .)

3. Because the new heavens and earth are a real place, there will be a form of time there. But thinking about never-ending time can be both exhausting and possibly boring. So talk with your family about those events you have been to where time seemed to fly (sports events, birthday parties, good movies, special events), and discuss why time seemed to go so quickly. Then relate that to how we might experience time in eternity.

4. Why not have a little family competition to see who can draw the most detailed picture of what a scene from the new heavens and earth might look like (remind family members of some of the physical details of the new earth we are told about in this chapter).

5. Myk suggests we could be able to either space travel or even time travel in eternity. Can your family members come up with any activities or experiences we might be able to do then that we can't now? Explain why you think this might be possible.

6. The best thing about eternity is spending it with the triune God. Have your family write out a prayer to God the Father, a prayer to God

the Son, and a prayer to God the Holy Spirit, thanking him for one specific aspect of our eternity to come.

Adults Study Guide

1. Talking about *three* heavens is confusing. Scholars find a variety of ways to get around this confusion. How might you distinguish between the atmosphere, God's current abode, and our final state (e.g., sky, heaven/paradise, new heavens and new earth; or sky, heaven, Heaven; or . . .)?

2. Myk made the statement that "Heaven is not in our space-time continuum." By this he meant you can't find God's current abode in a spaceship and the new heavens and earth will not simply by a continuation of space and time as we now know it. What movies or books might help our families grasp this idea a little? (The TARDIS could help, or episodes of *Star Trek*, or even Einstein's special theory of relativity . . .)

3. "Time flies" is a common expression. Discuss ways in which it seems that time flies and then relate that to how we might experience time in eternity.

4. How might we be asked to think of the New Jerusalem, with its thick walls, costly gates, and dazzling architecture? That is, in your own words describe what these images are telling us about our eternal home.

5. How would you respond to the question, "The city of Heaven is better than the garden of Eden"?

6. In what ways might we be able to make heaven on earth? And in what ways are we not able to make heaven on earth?

Chapter 3: Raised Immortal
(What Will We Be Like in the Resurrection?)

Family Study Guide

1. As a family or small group, plan a Communion service where prayers are offered and brief words are said that remind us that Christ's resurrection is the first-fruits of our own resurrection. If your family regularly takes Communion, perhaps do this as a small group; if, like Myk (he is a Baptist after all), your children are unbaptized, then you could still hold the service but instead of the bread and wine you could have crackers and grapes as a foretaste of communion.

2. Explain the similarities and differences between a physical and the spiritual body in light of 1 Corinthians 15:44.

3. Have each family member make a personal profile for one other family member listing what it is that makes the person unique (height, gender, personality, and so forth). Discuss how what it means to "be you" will continue for all eternity (i.e., discuss how personal identity is not lost in the resurrection).

4. Now discuss what aspects of your own personality might need to be either removed, refined, or redeemed, and how this might occur in the resurrection.

5. Discuss the question: Will we still have birthday parties on the new earth?

6. Have a discussion around the idea of children not being afraid in eternity because they will know their parents, other family, and friends, and will have a whole world of new friends to get to know. How does this make you feel? Does it answer any worries you might have about going to the new heavens and earth?

Adults Study Guide

1. At the next Communion service at church, meditate upon the fact that Christ's literal, physical resurrection is the first-fruits of your own, and talk afterwards about what difference that makes to your experience of Communion.

2. Explain the similarities and differences between a physical and the spiritual body in light of 1 Corinthians 15:44.

3. What things about yourself are fundamental in making you . . . well, you (i.e., physically, emotionally, psychologically, and so forth)? Discuss how these will be retained in the resurrection.

4. Now discuss what aspects of your own personality might need to be either removed, refined, or redeemed, and how this might occur in the resurrection. (For the very bold, you might like to ask others to contribute some of this information about yourself; just make sure they are *good* friends.)

5. Do you think we will age in the resurrection?

6. How might we think of the continuity of personal relationships into eternity? Think about spouses, children, family, friendships, and even

"enemies."

Chapter 4: An Endless Adventure
(What Will We Do in the New Jerusalem?)

Family Study Guide

1. Talk about the times when your family was the most relaxed. This might be a really special holiday or visits to grandparents, reading books together, or watching movies, and so forth.

2. What is it about relaxation that is so . . . well, relaxing? How might this be a partial image of what life is like in the New Jerusalem?

3. Now talk about the times when your family was the most active (in good ways). This might be playing sports, performing in a school play, working together doing chores (although that probably is not associated with fun by most children), and so forth.

4. What is it about constructive activity, especially creative activity, that is so rewarding? How might this be a partial image of what life is like in the New Jerusalem? Go around your family and discuss the projects each of you would most like to work on in the New Jerusalem.

5. Jason, age three, asked, "Are there toys in Heaven?" How might your family go about answering that?

6. Ed Strauss suggests we might have questions for some of the heroes of the faith and he lists six of his own. Make a list of questions your family wants to ask heroes of the faith.

Adults Study Guide

1. The biblical idea of rest is respite from enemies (especially sin). What things do you struggle with now that you will be relieved to know you won't have to struggle with in the New Jerusalem? (These could be internal or external things.)

2. What energizes you and puts spice into your life (e.g., sports, arts, hobbies, and so forth)? Do you think any of these will be a feature of the New Jerusalem? How?

3. How might the fact that we will still be working in eternity influence your view of work now?

4. The concept of rewards is not popular in our egalitarian world, and yet it is a central biblical idea. Discuss how might you cultivate eternal rewards in your daily life?

5. Name several events in your life that would not have been as enjoyable if you had not been able to share them with significant others. In relation to the public nature of enjoyment and the role our memories of these events plays, discuss ways in which eternity won't be boring.

6. Define the biblical concept of hope and relate that to eternity.

Chapter 5: A Great Cloud of Witnesses
(Who Will Be in Zion?)

Family Study Guide

1. Have you ever given much time to thinking about angels and demons? What do they do?

2. Zion is for those who love the Lord God. Discuss this as a family making clear that no one goes to Zion by accident or automatically, just because their parents will go there. (This would be a good time to have another discussion about what it means to be saved.)

3. Discuss what it means to "look like Christ" in our daily lives. (I.e., it doesn't mean we look like Christ physically, having to get a haircut like his and so forth. So what does it mean?)

4. How does following God's rules and commands and teachings make us truly free? You might like to talk about how following parents' rules makes for happier and healthier children, and so forth.

5. Sydney, age nine , asks, "How will we feel if people we love are not there?" Discuss as a family.

6. Talk about pets you have or have had and discuss their importance to your family. Now ask and answer the question as to whether or not pets will be in Zion.

Adults Study Guide

1. Have you ever given much time to thinking about angels and demons? What do they do?

2. Zion is "redemptive, fixed, and final," meaning that once there we will remain there for all eternity. How does that fact make you feel? What implications does this have for how we live now?

3. Hell has never been a popular topic, and that is especially so today. Do we really need to talk about and believe in the existence of Hell?

4. It will be impossible to sin in an eternity with God in Zion. Discuss what this means for our notions of moral freedom. How might this notion of freedom in Christ have implications for daily living?

5. Sydney, age nine, asks, "How will we feel if people we love are not there?" This is a really hard thing to think about. Discuss the options Myk presented in this chapter. Do you have a better solution than the one he came to?

6. What do you think about the possibility of some pets being in Zion? Is it possible or not?

Chapter 6: Conclusion: On Eating Pie in the Sky

Family Study Guide

1. As a family, make a list of five ways knowing about the new heavens and earth has practical consequences for your living now.

2. As a family, make a list of five ways in which we experience a foretaste of Heaven now (i.e., we feel God's love now, and so forth).

3. Attempt to put into everyday language your family will understand the following positions on the end times: despairing resignation, futurist activism, active anticipation. Discuss what each means and which one you want to cultivate.

4. Try to write a family position statement on how you will attempt to live in light of eternity. It might begin with, "Our family lives in light of eternity by: 1) enjoying God's presence in our lives. 2) . . ."

5. See if you can find examples of Christian songs that offer a positive view of life based on the hope we have within us to counter the negative examples of songs Myk provided in this final chapter. (Myk turns to Butterflyfish amongst others.)

6. To conclude, why not read to your children C. S. Lewis's *The Last Battle*, and finish with a prayer for God to kindle within our hearts a passion for his presence, his name, and for the future he is preparing for us.

Adults Study Guide

1. Discuss Donal Bloesch's claim that "Jesus came to bring not simply moral precepts but the reality of a new world order that revolutionizes the whole of life."

2. How does the "spiritual run ahead of the physical" when it comes to Heaven?

3. Of the three positions people adopt regarding the end times (despairing resignation, futurist activism, active anticipation), which one most accurately describes your own view before reading this book and

which one most accurately describes your view having now read this book?

4. Explain what it means to have *hope* according to a Christian (biblical) worldview.

5. If you are discussing this in a reading/book group, share with the group other Christian literature that paints the kind of anticipatory hope and love for God and his future that Myk so obviously finds in C. S. Lewis's *The Chronicles of Narnia*.

6. A good way to conclude might be to discuss the ways in which the Bible's teaching focuses on the *Eschatos* (Greek for the "Last One," Jesus Christ), not the *eschata* (Greek for the "last things").

Bibliography

Adler, Bill, ed. *Ask Billy Graham: The World's Best Loved Preacher Answers Your Most Important Questions*. Nashville: Thomas Nelson, 2007.

Alcorn, Randy. *Heaven*. Carol Stream, IL: Tyndale, 2004.

————. *Heaven: God's Answers to Your Every Need*. Carol Stream, IL: Tyndale, 2008.

Baillie, John. *And the Life Everlasting*. New York: Scribner, 1933.

Bird, Michael F. *Evangelical Theology: A Biblical and Systematic Introduction*. Grand Rapids: Zondervan, 2003.

Bloesch, Donald G. *The Last Things: Resurrection, Judgment, Glory*. Christian Foundations 7. Downers Grove: InterVarsity, 2004.

Burpo, Colton, Todd Burpo, and Sonja Burpo. *Heaven Is For Real for Kids*. Nashville: Tommy Nelson, 2011.

Burpo, Todd, and Lynn Vincent. *Heaven Is For Real: A Little Boy's Astounding Story of His Trip to Heaven and Back*. Nashville: W Publishing, 2010.

Calhoun, David, B. "The Hope of Heaven." In *Heaven*, edited by Christopher W. Morgan and Robert A. Peterson, 243–62. Theology in Community. Wheaton: Crossway, 2014.

Erickson, Millard J. *Christian Theology*. 2nd ed. Grand Rapids: Baker, 1998.

Fischer, John Martin. "Why Immortality Is Not So Bad." *International Journal of Philosophical Studies* 2 (1994) 262–67.

Grudem, Wayne. *Systematic Theology: An Introduction to Biblical Doctrine*. Leicester: InterVarsity; Grand Rapids: Zondervan, 1994.

Habets, Myk. *The Anointed Son: A Trinitarian Spirit Christology*. Eugene, OR: Pickwick, 2010.

————. "Disability and Divinization: Eschatological Parables and Allegations." In *Theology and the Experience of Disability: Perspectives from Voices Down Under*, edited by Andrew Picard and Myk Habets, 212–34. Abingdon: Ashgate, 2016.

————. "Naked but Not Disembodied: A Case for Anthropological Duality." *Pacific Journal of Baptist Research* 4/1 (2008) 33–50. http://www.baptistresearch.org.nz/uploads/6/2/0/4/6204774/pacific_journal_4-1_april_08.pdf.

————. "'Suffer the Little Children to Come to Me, for Theirs Is the Kingdom of Heaven.' Infant Salvation and the Destiny of the Severely Mentally Disabled." In *Evangelical Calvinism: Essays Resourcing the Continuing Reformation of the Church*, edited by Myk Habets and Robert Grow, 287–328. Princeton Theological Monographs. Eugene, OR: Pickwick, 2012.

Hewlett, Charles, and Joanne Hewlett. *Hurting Hope: What Parents Feel When Their Children Suffer*. London: Piquant, 2011.

Horton, Michael. *The Christian Faith: A Systematic Theology for Pilgrims on the Way*. Grand Rapids: Zondervan, 2011.

Kreeft, Peter J. *Everything You Wanted to Know About Heaven . . . But Never Dreamed of Asking*. San Francisco: Harper and Row, 1983.

Lewis, Clive S. *The Great Divorce*. C. S. Lewis Signature Classics. 1946. London: Collins, 2012.

―――. *The Last Battle*. The Chronicles of Narnia. New York: Collier, 1956.

―――. *The Last Battle*. The Chronicles of Narnia. London: HarperCollins, 1956.

―――. "Learning in War-Time." In *The Weight of Glory and Other Addresses*, edited by Walter Hooper, 20–32. London: Macmillan, 1980.

―――. *Mere Christianity*. C. S. Lewis Signature Classics. London: Collins, 2012.

―――. *Miracles*. The C. S. Lewis Signature Classics. 1947. London: Collins, 2012.

―――. *Out of the Silent Planet*. The Cosmic Trilogy. 1938. London: Harper Collins, 2005.

―――. *Perelandra [Voyage to Venus]*. The Cosmic Trilogy. 1943. London: HarperCollins, 2005.

―――. *The Problem of Pain*. C. S. Lewis Signature Classics. 1940. London: Collins, 2012.

―――. *Surprised by Joy*. New York: Harcourt, Brace/World, Harvest, 1955.

―――. "Transposition." In *Screwtape Proposes a Toast and Other Pieces*, 75–93. London: Fontana, 1965.

―――. *Voyage of the Dawn Treader*. New York: HarperCollins, 1994.

―――. "The Weight of Glory." In *Screwtape Proposes a Toast and Other Pieces*, 94–110. London: Fontana, 1965.

Lewis, Gordon R., and Bruce A. Demarest. *Integrative Theology: Historical, Biblical, Systematic, Apologetic, Practical*. 3 vols. in 1. Grand Rapids: Zondervan, 1996.

Lloyd-Jones, Sally. *The Jesus Storybook Bible*. Grand Rapids: Zondervan, 2007.

MacDonald, George. *Lilith*. 1895. Adelaide: eBooks at the University of Adelaide, 2014. https://ebooks.adelaide.edu.au/m/macdonald/george/lilith/complete.html.

―――. *Paul Faber, Surgeon*. 1878. http://www.online-literature.com/george-macdonald/paul-faber/51/.

Maclaren, Alexander. "Psalm 42.2, part 3." In *Maclaren's Commentary: Expositions of Holy Scripture*. N.p.: Demarva, 2013.

Malarkey, Alex. *The Boy Who Came Back from Heaven*. Carol Stream, IL: Tyndale House, 2010.

Martindale, Wayne. *Beyond the Shadowlands: C. S. Lewis on Heaven and Hell*. Wheaton: Crossway, 2005.

McBrien, Richard P. *Catholicism*. Vol. 2. Minneapolis: Winston, 1980.

McGrath, Alister E. *A Brief History of Heaven*. Oxford: Blackwell, 2003.

Middleton, J. Richard. *A New Heaven and a New Earth: Reclaiming Biblical Eschatology*. Grand Rapids: Baker, 2014.

Milne, Bruce. *Know the Truth: A Handbook of Christian Belief*. 3rd ed. Nottingham: InterVarsity, 2009.

―――. *The Message of Heaven and Hell*. BST. Leicester: InterVarsity, 2002.

Morgan, Christopher W., and Robert A. Peterson, eds. *Heaven*. Theology in Community. Wheaton: Crossway, 2014.

Pannenberg, Wolfhart. *What is Man? Contemporary Anthropology in Theological Perspective*. Translated by D. A. Priebe. Philadelphia: Fortress, 1970.

Peterson, Robert A. "Pictures of Heaven." In *Heaven*, edited by Christopher W. Morgan and Robert A. Peterson, 159–84. Theology in Community. Wheaton: Crossway, 2014.

Piper, John. *The Pleasures of God: Meditations on God's Delight in Being God*. Sisters, OR: Multnomah, 2000.

———. *The Purifying Power of Living by Faith in Future Grace*. Sisters, OR: Mulnomah, 1995.

Ramsey, Thor. *A Comedian's Guide to Theology*. Ventura, CA: Regal. 2008.

Reid, Gordon. "Afterword." In *The Wind from the Stars: Through the Year with George MacDonald*, edited by Gordon Reid, n.p. London: HarperCollins, 1992.

Robinson, Marilynne. *Gilead*. New York: Picador, 2004.

Rogers, Will. *A Connecticut Yankee*. 20th Century Fox, 1991.

Schwartz, Hans. *Eschatology*. Grand Rapids: Eerdmans, 2000.

Shelley, Marshall. "Two Minutes to Eternity." *Christianity Today*, July 11, 2011. http://www.christianitytoday.com/le/2011/july-online-only/minuteseternity.html.

Shriver, Maria. *What's Heaven?* New York: St. Martin's, 1999.

Strauss, Ed. *Heaven for Kids: My First Bible Reference for 5–8 Year Olds*. Uhrichsville, OH: Barbour, 2013.

Tada, Joni Erickson. *Heaven: Your Real Home*. Grand Rapids: Zondervan, 1995.

Thiselton, Anthony C. *Systematic Theology*. Grand Rapids: Eerdmans, 2015.

Tolkien, J. R. R. "Letter to Michael Tolkien, 9 June 1941." In *The Letters of J. R. R. Tolkien: A Selection*, edited by Humphrey Carpenter with the assistance of Christopher Tolkien, 55. Boston: Houghton Mifflin, 1981.

Toon, Peter. *Heaven and Hell: A Biblical and Theological Overview*. Nashville: Thomas Nelson, 1986.

Twelftree, Graham H. *Life after Death*. London: Monarch, 2002.

Weston, Tamara. "Pet Rocks." *Time*, December 23, 2010. http://content.time.com/time/specials/packages/article/0,28804,1947621_1947626_1947687,00.html.

Williams, C., ed. *The Letters of Evelyn Underhill*. London: Longmans, Green, 1943.

Wright, N. T. *New Heavens, New Earth: The Biblical Picture of the Christian Hope*. Grove Biblical Series B11. Cambridge: Grove, 1999.

Wright, Tom. *Surprised by Hope*. London: SPCK, 2007.

Zaleski, Carol. "In Defence of Immortality." *First Things* 105 (August–September 2000) 42.

Index

abode, 13, 34, 115–16
achieve, 51–52
achieved, 68, 72, 77
achievement, 72
adult, ix, 32, 69, 77, 90, 95
adulthood, 45
adults, 114, 116, 118–19, 121, 123
age, 2–3, 45–48, 57, 68, 97, 101,
    118–19, 121–22
ageless, 46, 57
aging, 45–46, 49, 54
alcohol, 67, 100–101
androgynous, 48
angel, 16, 22, 25, 48, 53, 64, 82–87,
    96, 121
angelic, 82–83
angelos, 82
angels, 13, 82–84, 104
animal, 3, 27, 32, 44, 47, 70, 74, 82,
    87, 90–97
animals, 93
ankles, 52
anticipated, 59
anticipation, 75, 102, 111, 123
anticipatory, 124
antlers, 95
apples, 65
archangel, 83
architecture, 21, 33, 116
artisans, 76
artist, 34, 55, 71, 75, 78–79
Aslan, 30, 58, 109

barbeque, 42, 91
beasts, 27, 81, 93
beautiful, 28, 56, 58, 71, 76, 103
beautifully, 22, 77, 110
beauty, 1, 5, 20–21, 28, 32, 43, 50, 66,
    70, 106
beer, 17
belief, 7, 14, 24, 29, 37, 44–45, 71, 126
believe, 4–5, 34–37, 41–43, 45–46,
    48–49, 51, 55–56, 65, 69, 71,
    76, 82, 90, 92–94, 99, 106–7,
    114, 121
believed, 100
believer, 13, 18, 22, 24–25, 34, 38, 44,
    47, 51–52, 59–60, 62–64, 82,
    85–87, 89, 92–93, 97, 99–100
believing, 34, 103
belong, 31, 53, 103
belonging, 23–24
beloved, 49
bodily, 16, 19, 37–38, 40–43, 49, 57,
    59, 87
body, 3, 8, 10, 13–14, 16, 19, 22,
    27–28, 37–48, 50–52, 56–57,
    59, 62, 75, 83, 86, 88, 92–93,
    100, 105, 117–18
bones, 42, 104
boredom, 68
boring, 67–68, 70–72, 115, 120
build, 62, 99
builder, 16, 62, 71, 75
building, 5, 24–25, 27, 62, 108
built, 21, 31, 62, 72, 74, 100

cherubim, 83
cherubs, 2, 9, 19, 27
childhood, 4, 33, 46, 57
children, 45, 54, 96, 99, 125–26
chocolate, 49
Christ, v, 4–5, 9–10, 13–18, 20–26,
    30, 33, 37–46, 49, 51–52,
    54–57, 61–67, 71–77, 79–80,
    82, 85–89, 92–93, 96, 99,
    101–2, 106–9, 111, 117–18,
    121–22, 124
city, 15–17, 19–25, 27, 31, 37, 47,
    52–53, 65, 70, 80, 82, 92, 100,
    108, 110, 116
clothes, 42
comedian, 48, 127
communion, 16, 22, 32, 38, 117–118
community, 5, 9, 48, 52, 73, 92,
    125–27
companions, x, 74, 87, 90, 93–95
company, 31, 46–47, 57, 79
cried, 30–31, 61, 69, 107
crown, 12, 63–64, 70, 85
crowning, 66
Crowns, 12
cry, 48, 69, 104–5, 107–8
crying, 22, 106–7, 110
cultural, 74, 80
culture, 56, 73–75, 92, 97, 101, 103

decay, 14, 19, 26, 44, 86, 93
delight, ix, 32, 34, 65, 73, 75, 77,
    79–80, 89–90, 94, 127
delighted, 60, 79
delightful, 3, 28
desire, 49, 64, 76–78, 88, 91, 101, 109
disability, 40, 44–45, 55–57, 125
disabled, 44, 107, 125
disembodied, 2, 15, 38, 42, 57, 125
divinization, 45, 125
drink, 19, 24, 32, 38, 65–67, 77, 95
drinking, 65–67, 80

eat, 19, 38, 49, 65, 67, 90–91, 95
eaten, 44
eating, vii, 43, 49, 65–67, 80, 98, 123
embodied, 38–39, 42, 52, 81

embodiment, 46
embody, 92
embrace, 5, 74
endless, vii, 20, 28, 58, 66, 68, 71, 95,
    119
endlessly, 68
enjoy, 6–7, 10, 25, 32, 45, 48, 52, 60,
    62–63, 67, 70, 75, 79
enjoyable, 31, 69, 120
enjoyed, 3, 8, 27, 100
enjoying, 3, 63, 69, 123
environment, 17, 19–20, 24, 29, 35,
    74, 80
eternal, v, 2, 13–15, 20, 23–24, 28–29,
    38, 48, 52, 54, 56, 59, 61–62,
    65–66, 70, 72, 78, 85–87, 89,
    92, 95–96, 109, 116, 120
eternally, 61, 86, 92
eternity, 12, 15, 20, 31, 33, 41, 45, 49,
    52, 54, 57, 59, 64–72, 74–75,
    78–79, 89, 102–3, 106–8,
    115–18, 120–23, 127
everlasting, 36, 38, 68, 78, 108, 125
excited, 96
excitement, 28, 70
exciting, 2, 9, 35, 37, 50–51, 59, 67,
    70, 80
exploration, 31, 66, 70
explore, 29, 31, 37
explored, 27, 57
exploring, 31, 65, 80
eye, x, 4–5, 21, 27–28, 33, 39, 71, 90,
    95, 99, 105–6, 110

faith, v, ix, 4–7, 9, 13, 23–26, 38, 62,
    71–72, 74, 86–87, 89, 101–2,
    105–7, 111, 119, 126–27
faithful, 2, 8, 24, 30, 55, 63, 73, 77, 79,
    84, 91, 107
faithfully, 6, 14, 92, 96
faithfulness, 61
fall, 6, 25, 28, 37, 44, 52, 54, 88, 94,
    106–107
fallen, 26, 38–39, 46, 55, 64, 84–86,
    96, 101, 107
fallenness, 72
falling, 52–53, 56

family, ix–x, 4, 9, 11, 30, 47, 67–69,
        76, 92, 96, 108, 113, 115–19,
        121, 123
flesh, 29, 38–39, 42, 44, 57, 60, 76, 91
friend, ix-x, 6, 8, 11, 23, 33, 46–47,
        54, 67, 69, 81, 86, 89, 95, 105,
        109, 117–18
friends, 23
friendships, 118

gender, 57, 117
gendered, 48

Habets, iii-iv, x, 15, 45, 88, 125
happiness, 43, 79, 89, 92
happy, 2–3, 58, 61, 89, 95, 98,
        104–105
harps, 9, 12, 19, 27, 70
Heaven, i, iii-iv, vii, ix, 1–3, 6–35,
        37–43, 45–48, 50–54, 56–72,
        74–82, 85–96, 98–105, 108–
        11, 113–17, 119, 123, 125–27
heavenly, 2, 13, 16, 25, 48, 63–66, 82,
        85, 87, 99, 108
heavens, 29, 127
hell, 2, 14–15, 21, 25, 37, 52, 56, 67,
        74, 85–87, 89, 102, 105, 121,
        126–27
human, 4, 10, 16, 19, 26, 31–32, 40,
        42–43, 46, 48–50, 56, 61,
        64–67, 72, 75, 80, 82–84, 88,
        95–96, 98, 100, 102
humanity, ix, 9, 41–42, 60, 63, 65, 74,
        84, 90, 92–93, 95, 102
humans, 20, 26, 40, 42, 44, 52–53, 80,
        84–86, 90–91, 93, 97

imagination, 2, 6–8, 16–17, 27,
        31–32, 45, 52, 74–75, 96, 100,
        111, 113–14
immoral, 64
immortal, vii, 36, 43, 52, 67, 85, 96,
        117
immortality, 38, 67–68, 85, 93, 96,
        100, 125, 127
individual, 21, 40, 42, 57, 92
individuality, 41
infant, 45–46, 57, 125

infinite, 49, 70, 77, 84
infinitely, 34, 69
infinity, 12, 20, 69
intercourse, 48
intermediate, 14–15, 33, 48
Israel, 21, 25, 65, 100
Israelites, 18, 23

Jerusalem, vii, 17, 19, 21–22, 24–25,
        46, 48, 58, 60, 62, 74, 80, 110,
        116, 119
Jesus, 3–4, 6–7, 13, 15–16, 18–21,
        23–25, 37–38, 41–43, 46, 48,
        52, 54, 56–57, 60, 62–63, 65,
        67, 71–72, 74, 76–77, 85–89,
        91, 98, 100, 102, 106–9,
        123–24, 126
judge, 14, 64–65
judged, 62, 64, 86
judging, 39, 64–65, 78
judgment, 15, 51, 62–64, 84, 86, 90,
        125

ladybug, 28
lamb, 17, 19, 22, 24, 73, 86, 90
language, 4, 6, 14–16, 24–26, 42,
        73–74, 92, 123
learning, ix, 43, 49, 59, 65, 68, 78,
        80, 126
leopards, 90
Leviathan, 94
Liam, v, 78
lion, 58, 83, 90–91

marriage, 19, 48–49
married, 48–50
memories, 69
memory, 68–70, 105, 120
Moa, 94
music, 2, 5, 12, 27–28, 76, 105–6, 115
Musical, 12
Musically, 53
Musician, 53

Odele, 49

peace, 23, 26, 60, 70, 77, 89–90
peaceful, 32

pet, 4, 14, 17, 19, 22, 26, 33, 61, 63,
    82, 85, 87, 90–93, 95–97, 100,
    121–22, 127
play, 4, 9, 29, 32, 41, 46, 51–52,
    54–55, 57, 72–73, 75–76, 80,
    91–92, 99, 119–20
played, 53
playful, 11, 57
playfully, 63
playing, 9, 12, 51, 57, 65, 71, 79–80,
    87, 119
pleasure, 5, 20, 32, 43, 45, 49, 64,
    68–70, 72, 75, 79, 109–10
pleasures, 34, 127
priest, 4–5, 11, 21, 113–14
priesthood, 3, 5
priestly, 4–6, 8
procreation, 48

race, 60, 70
rainbow, 5, 75, 81
recognition, 47, 79
recognize, 40, 43, 47, 54–55, 57
recognized, 47
Reepicheep, 109
rest, 8, 10, 55, 59–61, 64–66, 70, 72,
    77, 80, 92, 99, 107, 119
rested, 60
restful, 51
resting, 2, 59–60, 65, 79–80
resurrect, 41
resurrected, 10, 13–14, 20, 22, 26–27,
    37–38, 40–46, 48–49, 51–52,
    54, 56–57, 59, 85–86, 88, 93
resurrection, vii, 6–7, 13–16, 19, 23,
    26, 34, 36–57, 60–62, 64–65,
    70, 72, 76, 81, 85–90, 92, 100,
    102–3, 107–8, 117–18, 125
reward, 61–65, 77–78, 110, 120
rewarded, 62–63
rewarding, 73, 119
rewards, 63–64, 77

Satan, 84–86, 96
sex, 43, 48–49, 77
sexual, 48–49
sheep, 47, 84, 90

sheepdog, 54
sing, 5, 28, 53, 60, 74, 76, 95, 104
singers, 100
singing, 60, 103
sky, vii, 16, 31–33, 75, 98, 100, 106,
    115–16, 123
sleep, 51, 107
smell, 24, 27, 31, 47, 54, 56, 75
sorrow, 103, 106, 109
space, 8, 16–17, 20, 24, 31–35, 38, 69,
    115–16
suffer, 45, 61–62, 86, 105, 125–26
suffering, 26, 40, 94, 106
sun, 17–18, 20, 22, 30, 33, 53, 73
swim, 109
swimming, 19
Sydney, v, 51, 69, 74, 121–122

taste, 31–32, 54, 67, 75
time, 4–5, 7–8, 14, 16–18, 20, 22–26,
    28, 31–39, 41, 43, 46–49, 51–
    53, 55–56, 60, 62–63, 67–69,
    71–76, 80, 82–88, 90, 93–96,
    99–102, 107, 110–11, 115–16,
    119, 121, 123, 126–27
timeless, 20
timelessness, 12
transform, 32, 37, 78, 80
transformation, 39, 54
transformed, 18, 25, 39, 43
travel, 10, 31, 33, 115
traveling, 33, 69

work, x, 4, 6–9, 24, 28–30, 36, 41, 52,
    55, 59–64, 66, 70–71, 73–74,
    77, 79–81, 85–86, 94, 99–101,
    106, 108–9, 119–20
working, 26, 29, 51, 54, 65, 74–76,
    79–80, 109, 119–20
worship, 2, 14, 25, 36, 60–61, 71, 74,
    76–77, 80, 83, 108
worshipping, 60, 79, 92

zebra, 95